SARATOGA

SARATOGA

AMERICA'S BATTLEFIELD

Timothy Holmes (signature)

Libby Smith-Holmes (signature)

TIMOTHY HOLMES & LIBBY SMITH-HOLMES

Charleston · London

THE
History
PRESS

Published by The History Press
Charleston, SC 29403
www.historypress.net

Cover images: Cannon images courtesy of Saratoga National Historic Park; Ellen Hardin Walworth image courtesy of Saratoga Springs History Museum; monument image courtesy of Saratoga Springs History Museum.

First published 2012

Manufactured in the United States

ISBN 978.1.60949.336.3

Library of Congress CIP data applied for.

Contents

CONTENTS

Acknowledgements

Thanks go out to the following, all of whom aided so much during this project:

The helpful and resourceful staff of Saratoga National Historical Park (SNHP), especially Superintendent Joe Finan, Chief of Interpretation and Visitor Services Gina Johnson, Curator Christine Valosin, Park Ranger/Historian Eric Schnitzer, Park Ranger Bill Valosin and eminent veteran ranger Joe Craig.

The indispensable personnel at the Saratoga Room in the Saratoga Springs Public Library.

James Parillo, executive director of the Saratoga Springs History Museum.

The scholars and writers who have gone before. An application was recently submitted for the Park to gain listing on the National Register of Historic Places. To ensure accuracy in narrating the story of the Saratoga battles, I reproduce some of it here, with the park's kind permission. The writers drew information from *Decision on the Hudson: The Battles of Saratoga* by John Luzader. The book's 2002 reissue benefited from the meticulous overview of the Battlefield's Ranger-Historian Eric Schnitzer.

The scholars, researchers and writers who preserve, transcribe and share the data and interpretation of original materials.

Those who learn and apply the lessons of the battles of Saratoga to champion the freedoms gained.

Leadership is always important. SNHP ("the Battlefield") has been fortunate with consistently capable and forward-thinking superintendents. Most recently, Superintendent Joe Finan made great strides toward implementing the plans of many.

Special thanks to image sources: Saratoga National Historical Park (SNHP), West Point Museum (WPM), Saratoga Springs History Museum (SSHM), Skidmore College's Alex Chaucer and Leandra Cooper (Chaucer/Cooper) and Benson Lossing's *Field Book* (Lossing).

Those not named here will be thanked personally.

Introduction

The Telling of History

This book takes into consideration how the story was told from the time of the epic event that defined the region.

The future belongs to those who will come. The telling of our stories to date will help to shape their perception and connection. The viewpoints, words and ways of expression of earlier storytellers have been included. It is hoped that the long trajectory of thinking on this subject will add perspective.

An important purpose of the book is to connect the reader with resources for current and updated information and thoughts on the topics related to the battles of Saratoga.

Chapter 1

The Prelude

Just twelve years before the "shot heard 'round the world" at Lexington and Concord, British North America was secured for the future. With the capitulation of France in 1763 after the Seven Years' War and the end of the French and Indian Wars that had raged for seventy years, peace was ensured. The eastern seaboard of North America from Nova Scotia to Georgia was safely English at last.

The colonists in America could now continue to break the wilderness and build better lives for their families and communities without the threat of military action and marauding bands from Canada. A strong but compassionate King George III would oversee growth of ports and production for the empire through his singularly enterprising subjects in the New World. Or so it seemed.

REGION OF CHANGE—CORRIDOR OF DESTINY

Ancient tectonic and geological activity had formed mountain chains running northeasterly from today's Deep South to Canada, as well as seams of lakes. Straddling the territories of the colonies of New York and Quebec, the lake called Lac du Saint Sacrament (later Champlain) was an exceptionally long body of water that served significantly in providing a landscape for the contest of empires.

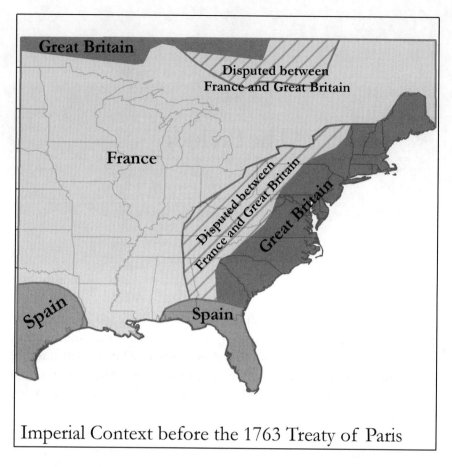

Imperial Context before the 1763 Treaty of Paris

The water and land corridor from Montreal to New York City was the scene of constant skirmishes between nations vying for power in North America. *Chaucer/Cooper.*

Between the Adirondack dome/Appalachian chain and the ranges of the Green and White Mountains of the Hampshire Grants—which would become Vermont—lie the waters and trails that had served as highways for the first Americans. Archaeology confirms thousands of years of human activity in the network of pathways on land and in the waterways where seasonal migrations and hunting grounds continued to define the cultures and lifetimes of the native population.

Historical Context

France and Holland

The interest of France in North America developed in parallel to that of Britain, Holland and Spain from the earliest days of European discovery of the New World. After a century of expeditions searching determinedly for, and sometimes finding, portable wealth such as gold and furs, the imperial European kingdoms began to pin down ownership claims in earnest.

In 1609, two expeditions set into motion a contest for the continent that centered on the Champlain-Hudson Valley. Skirmishes, battles and wars would go on until the new United States of America had won its arduous revolution 175 years later. Samuel de Champlain sailed for France and claimed the territory around the lake that would later be given his name. Henry Hudson, an Englishman in the employ of Holland, guided his eighty-five-foot, three-masted Dutch ship *Halfmoon* up a broad river in search of the Northwest Passage to the Orient. In later generations, the river would be called the Hudson and a northern interior shore named for his ship. Just sixty miles apart, the two men, working for countries utterly opposed in their competition to gain control of the new continent, were unaware of each other's presence.

As with all beginnings, fateful strokes scripted histories that were destined to come. Champlain put on a display of his firepower, killing a small number of Mohawks. Until the ejection of New France from North America, the large and complex Iroquois Confederacy to which the slain Mohawks belonged became the declared enemy of France. The planting of the flag for Holland at the juncture of two great rivers (now called Hudson and Mohawk) established the Dutch as arbiters of what would occur in this north country for generations to come.

Struggle for territory was part of the fabric of the New World. The unrecorded history through thousands of years wove and rent factions and tribes. Into this world entered the ambitious colonizers. In the early period, the waterways were most important for travel; controlling them was paramount. As land was defined and deeded, the first ten to fifteen miles on each side of a waterway was the important part. At certain intersecting points of well-traveled routes, destiny repeatedly played a hand.[1]

Britain

By 1664, England was a monarchy once more, under Charles II. The experiment of England as a republic had ended after a bloody civil war, allowing the redirection of national military energies outward to continue exploration and conquest. New Amsterdam was taken and renamed New York. However, in New York and Albany, which had been trading posts since 1614 and permanently settled since about 1623, Dutch traditions of law and culture continued under English rule.

For years, the warriors of the Iroquois Five Nations had harassed the French settlements in Canada. Now the French began to strike back in organized force. A war party of six hundred Frenchmen and Algonquin Indians worked its way south toward the Mohawk settlements in the winter of 1665–66. The men emerged from the woods at Schenectady and into a Mohawk ambush, precipitating a retreat to Quebec.

A new expedition of 1,300 men and two cannons went forth on the long journey from Quebec in October 1666, destroyed the Mohawk Castles and raised the flag, claiming this area of New York for King and France.

The French and the Mohawks stayed apart until stirred by an attack on villages of the Seneca, a member group of the Iroquois Confederacy. In 1689, a strong war party of about 250 canoes with 1,300 warriors retaliated, ascending to the settlements of Montreal and destroying all except for trophies taken home along the Saratoga trail. In the same year of 1689, war was declared between France and England. The accession to the English throne of William III via the "Glorious Revolution" consolidated the empowerment of Parliament and confirmed England as a Protestant country. William's origin and kinship with Dutch princely houses meant a shift in the balance of political and religious power in Europe that the French king could not tolerate.

ENGLISH FORTIFICATION OF SARATOGA

Two strong creeks, the Battenkill and Fish Creek, enter the great Hudson River within half a mile of each other in an area the Mohawks called Saratoga ("the great hillside beside the swift waters"). An island in the river provided a good fording place. The first Americans knew it as a good location for settlement for about twelve thousand years; Europeans recognized its strategic military value by building a series of forts near the Saratoga settlement between 1689 and 1763 to protect the northern strongholds of Albany and Schenectady from anticipated raids and incursions.

The news of the threat was delivered to Albany:

> *At a Convention &c Albany 21 August 1689*
> *Resolved to acquaint ye Inhabitants of ye County ye news yt we received of Col Pynchen*
> *   That Pemmaquid was taken by ye Indians and French 45 People kild & taken—also that there should be a ship be come to Quebek of ye French with news of wars Between Engld & france & therefore nothing can be Expected but yt ye French will doe all ye mischieffe they can to this governmt & therefore every one to be upon there guarde & take care they be not surprized[2]*

1689: Fort Vrooman

After the taking of New Amsterdam in 1664, the region's Dutch settlers had peacefully transferred loyalty to the English, participating with them in colonial militias. King William's War (1689–97) was the first of six colonial conflicts between France and England, the start of seventy years of sporadic and intense fighting for supremacy in North America. Fort Vrooman, a fortified homestead, was built in 1689 around the house of Bartel Vrooman at Saratoga, south of Fish Creek on the west side of the river. The resolves continued:

> *Upon ye news yt three People should be kild at Bartel Vromans at Sarachtoge by ye Indians*
> *Resolved by Convention yt Leift Jochim Staets forwith goe with ten men to Sarachtoge to see how ye matter is, & bring us an accompt with ye first & yt he Cito send a Post hither with ye tideings…[3]*

> *Resolved that there be a fort made about ye house of Bartel Vroman at Sarachtoge & Twelve men Raised out of ye Two Companies of ye Citty*

*& 2 Companies of ye County to lye there upon pay who are to have
12d a day besides Provisions and some Indians of Skachkook to be there
with them to goe out as skouts in yt Part of ye County.*[4]

Parties of men with Schaghticoke Indians were kept there to protect
the settlers and patrol the country to the north. It was used also in August
1690, during the first expedition against Canada, by a party of 515 men
from New York, Connecticut and Maryland led by Fitz John Winthrop
of Connecticut and Johannes Schuyler of Albany. The fortification was
not maintained, and only a few families ventured to make their homes in
the area over the subsequent twenty years.

During Queen Anne's War in 1709, a stockade fort was built on the
east bank of the river, guarding the ford just below the island. It was one
of a series made by a 1,500-man army on the march for Montreal. In
1711, it was left as the northernmost military post when forts to the north
were burned following another failed campaign to Quebec.

In response to France extending its frontier south with activities along
both shores of Lake Champlain, a fort was built under Philip Livingston
in September and October 1721, most likely at the Vrooman site.
Records show work done in 1739 and a 1745 rebuilding of the Livingston
fortification that completed a square stockade fort with a blockhouse on
each corner, capable of supporting about two hundred troops. With the
outbreak of King George's War (1744–48), Saratoga was strengthened
as a strategic point in the Hudson Valley, while the British went on the
offensive. The first conquest of Louisbourg, France's "Gibraltar of North
America" on Cape Breton (June 15, 1745), made the English settlements
in the Champlain-Hudson Valley targets in the path of reprisal.

On the night of November 27, 1745, a war party of 280 French and 229
Indians from Fort St. Frederic (Crown Point, New York) caught Saratoga
entirely by surprise. The village was undefended and the fort virtually
empty. Instead of installing a French detachment at Fort Saratoga, they
burned the fort, houses and mills, killed and scalped thirty inhabitants
and took the rest of the settlement's inhabitants prisoner.

Through the winter of 1745–46, the fort was rebuilt at twice the size
and renamed Fort Clinton in honor of the new colonial governor of New
York. The region was subject to frequent forays of French and Indian
expeditions. On April 7, 1747, a party of British soldiers was ambushed

between Fort Clinton and Fish Creek by sixty Frenchmen and Indians. Six or eight men were killed and a number taken prisoner. In early June, an expeditionary force from Fort St. Frederic (Crown Point) again succeeded, capturing a detachment of one hundred New York soldiers from Fort Clinton in the area between Saratoga and Lake Champlain. At the end of June 1747, a formidable force of French soldiers and Abenaki, Sauk and Nepissing warriors concentrated at the Great Carrying Place (Fort Edward) and harassed Fort Clinton, taking at least forty prisoners and twenty-eight scalps. However, efforts to set the blockhouses afire were defeated. The French force returned to Lake Champlain.

The provisioning of colonial troops was erratic. Colonel Peter Schuyler, who had brought a regiment up from New Jersey, was advised by the governor to stop paying his men out of his own resources for fear that other regiments would mutiny out of discontent. On September 20, 1747, the garrison marched out, leaving Fort Clinton undefended. The New York governor and assembly were continuously in disagreement on conducting effective offensive campaigns against Canada. The forts at Saratoga fell victim to this disorganization and were dismantled and burned under the governor's orders in October 1747, leaving Fort Clinton's twenty chimneys standing. Along with the fort went the stockade on the east bank of the river. With the massacre of 1745 still fresh in memory, little development took place in the Saratoga area.

A new fort at Saratoga, planned on an expansive scale to serve as a concentration and staging area for troops, munitions and supplies, was named in honor of Sir Charles Hardy, governor of the New York colony. Work on Fort Hardy began on August 19, 1757, said to have covered fifteen acres on the northwest corner of the junction of Fish Creek and the Hudson River. It commanded a river crossing point at the south end of the island. The barracks for the soldiers were 220 feet long, and three extensive storage buildings had a capacity for three thousand barrels of flour.

Of the following seventy-four years, thirty-three were spent in the shadow and impact of European war. Attacks from the French and their Algonquin allies of Canada remained an ongoing threat.

COLONIAL DISCONTENT GROWS, 1763–1775

In the twelve years between the British triumph over the French empire in North America and the triggering of the American Revolution, changes of mutual perception and affection between king and colonies came fast.

King George III took the throne in 1760 following the death of his grandfather. George III was to be the last English monarch to attempt full command of the government. The power of Parliament had steadily grown in preceding centuries; the English civil war one hundred years earlier had made a case for mistrusting parliamentary power on a representative basis. This king, the first of the Hanoverians to be fully English-bred, preferred the concept of full power from the top down. Leaders of Parliament largely obliged him.

In the thirteen colonies, the exercise of power in governance was becoming a practical reality. From Massachusetts to Virginia, the sixth generation of colonists was managing successful sustenance and development. Each colony had its own working governing body that carried out the routine policies of the government in London.

Treaty of Paris 1763

Boundaries of the empires, 1763–75, superimposed on today's map. *Chaucer/ Cooper.*

The removal of the threat of New France had effects in London, though undetected at first. Along with the sense of security came a new sense of confidence. The colonial population, largely rural and on or near the frontier, had developed a toughness and self-reliance that set it apart from its European origins. The rigors of cutting and clearing and of laying out the fundamentals of community again and again began to give definition to the sort of people it would take to succeed in making their way on the vast continent. Already there was impatience to go on into "the back country" to the west of the long frontier.

The widening gulf of understanding came to a marked conflict in the case of the Stamp Act. The government in London, realizing the extraordinary

The Stamp Act, passed by Parliament in 1765, affected all American colonists and required them to pay a tax on every piece of printed paper they used, the revenues being used to help pay the costs of defending and protecting the American frontier near the Appalachian Mountains. The colonists viewed the Stamp Act as a direct attempt by England to raise money in the colonies without the approval of the colonial legislatures—taxation without representation. *Lossing.*

cost of the Seven Years' War in North America, sought recovery with a tax on paper used in commercial transactions and printed materials such as newspapers and magazines. An added expense to be covered by stamped paper—and stirring concern among colonists—was the further maintenance of troops in North America. The Stamp Act was not the first such impost: the Molasses Tax, aimed at moderating and gaining from the trade of the North American colonies with the West Indies, had been accepted by the practitioners of commerce in the Americas. The perception of the implications of the Stamp Act, seen not only as burdensome in itself but also as a dangerous precedent, reflected a new and different sense of relationship with "the mother country." The colonists enjoyed rights and freedoms largely considered "English" but did not pair gratitude with these privileges when taxes were imposed with little recourse.

The king's view of his subjects, framed in paternalistic familial terms, was of a benign father caring for his children but ready to punish any who acted rebelliously. He expected obedience and respect and was first disappointed and then outraged when the "children" failed to behave with proper submission to his authority.

THE SARATOGA PATENT

The Schuyler family members were some of the Dutch proprietors who benefited from coming onto the scene early. With some considerable risk and skill, they along with other Dutch families had settled the core of the Hudson River Valley. Above Albany, the frontier was unclearly defined—but therefore full of opportunity.

First the Dutch and then the English attempted to gain control of land by bargain and purchase from the resident Indians. There were apparent differences of understanding on each side regarding the implications of the resulting documents. This resulted in years of delay in the establishment of a settlement by the Europeans.

A major holding for the Schuyler family lay within the Saratoga Patent, negotiated in 1684 and confirmed by the colonial government in 1708. Principals included Colonel Peter Schuyler, Johannes Schuyler, Robert Livingston and several others. The Saratoga Patent lay to the north of Albany and on both sides of the great north river, the Hudson. A most

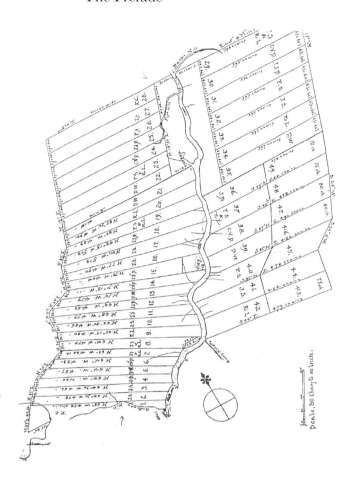

The portion of the
Saratoga Patent
embracing the
Hudson River
in the Battlefield
area. *SNHP.*

valuable portion lay along the riverbanks. Here the Schuylers established
and developed large tracts of land for lumbering and agriculture and the
raising of livestock. This large swath of land was Saratoga.

During the long period of struggle between French and English in
the vast territories north of Albany, activity was concentrated around
settlements along the riverbanks, and Saratoga was the northern
periphery for the centers of Albany and Schenectady.

Despite the disruptions, the landholders held on and continued to
develop their pursuits. Forest clearing and planting progressed. The
Schuylers became advanced practitioners in raising flax and processing it
into linen. Industry flourished in the form of their lumber and flax mills
along Fish Creek at Saratoga.

The Schuyler properties extended to what became known as Bemis Heights, eight miles south of the Saratoga settlement. After the peace of 1763, tenant farmers were making inroads in the ancient forest and setting up farming operations on the tableland overlooking the river.

PROGRESS AFTER 1763

With the capitulation of the French in 1763, the uncertainty ended. With the north country under one flag, it was possible to think about a reliable future. More settlers came to clear land and establish farms. Those who

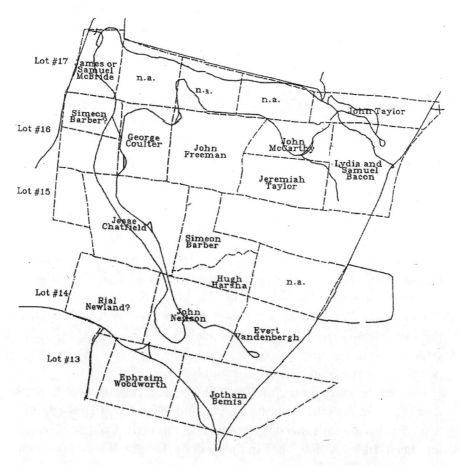

Schuyler's farm lessees in 1777 (draft in a SNHP Cultural Landscape Report, 1995).

took the opportunity to go frontiering in this way worked under the lease system. For annual rent of produce or labor, a family was able to farm, first for subsistence and then for gain. Under this system, tenant farmers might be able to save money toward the purchase of their own land.

Two such men were John Freeman and John Neilson. While they settled under a state of peace on Schuyler land shortly before 1777, their destinies were to diverge widely. In 1769, John Freeman leased 170 acres in Great Lott 16, built a house and barn and cleared 60 acres for crops. John Neilson, born in New Jersey in 1753, traveled north in the spring of 1772 and found a place to settle at Bemis Heights. He worked his way to saving enough money to purchase land on Bemis Heights and set to clearing and farming.

The stage was set for great events at this ordinary place.

Chapter 2

The Battles of Saratoga, 1777

THE MILITARY SITUATION TO 1777

The prospects for American independence were grim as the military campaign season of 1777 approached. A string of recent defeats exposed the weaknesses of the inexperienced and undermanned Continental army in the face of the well-trained British forces and made distant the memories of American victories in 1775 at Lexington and Concord, Fort Ticonderoga and Bunker Hill. In the Northern Department, under the command of General Philip Schuyler, an ill-conceived operation against Canada aimed at driving the British out and drawing French Canadians to the cause resulted in defeat at Quebec City in December 1775.

As the tattered remnants of the American forces led by Benedict Arnold attempted to lay siege to the city, some four thousand troops under the command of General John Burgoyne reinforced Sir Guy Carleton, governor and commanding general of the British forces in Canada. Carleton mounted a counteroffensive in June 1776 that drove the Americans out of Canada and into the southern end of the Champlain Valley. He then began preparations for a naval assault on the American strongholds at Crown Point and Fort Ticonderoga. Once the forts were captured, he intended to cross over to the Hudson River, capture Albany and establish communications with General William Howe's army in New York City.

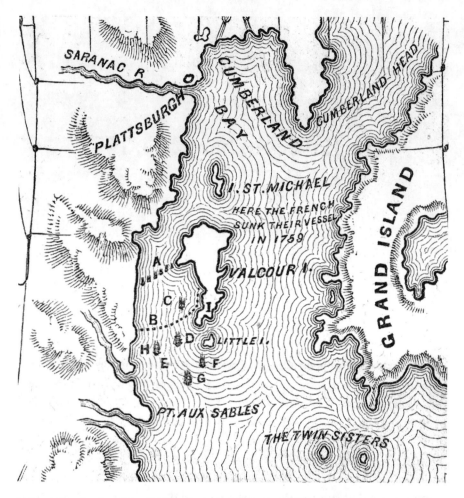

Valcour Bay, the site of the 1776 battle, is now a National Historic Landmark, as is the USS *Philadelphia*, which sank shortly after the October 11 battle and was raised in 1935. Many American ships and small boats were sunk intentionally to keep them out of the hands of the British. In 1997, another pristine underwater wreck was located during a survey by the Lake Champlain Maritime Museum. Two years later, it was conclusively identified as the gundalow *Spitfire*; this site was listed on the National Register in 2008. *Lossing.*

On July 7, during an American council of war attended by Generals Benedict Arnold, Horatio Gates and John Sullivan, Schuyler made the decision to assemble a flotilla at Skenesborough (now Whitehall), New York, to meet the threat and placed Arnold in command. On October 11, Arnold's makeshift navy met the advancing British off Valcour Island, just south of Plattsburgh, New York. While the battle (which constituted the first naval engagement of the war) resulted in the loss of all the American ships and forced Arnold's retreat overland to Fort Ticonderoga, it served to stall Carleton's advance. Within a week, an early snowfall induced Carleton to abandon the operation and return to Canada for the winter. For Burgoyne, who had accompanied Carleton, the expedition produced disappointment in the abilities of Carleton but reinforced his opinion of the strategic value in gaining control of the upper Hudson. He left for London in December to attend to his duties as a member of Parliament and to lobby for a renewal of the campaign to be launched under his command the following year.

While Schuyler's Northern Department was struggling to turn back Carleton's advance, the main body of the Continental army under George Washington was unable to prevent Howe from taking New York City. After landing at Staten Island on July 3, 1776, with more than twenty thousand troops transported by a powerful flotilla commanded by his brother, Richard, Lord Howe, William Howe defeated Washington in a series of battles that forced the Americans to retreat west into Pennsylvania. Washington's subsequent victories at Trenton (December 26, 1776) and Princeton (January 3, 1777) did much to revive the hopes of the American cause, but the British clearly held the initiative in all theaters of the war when the opposing forces went into winter quarters.

PLANNING FOR THE HUDSON RIVER CAMPAIGN

The British high command spent the winter months of 1777 developing plans for upcoming operations that it hoped would result in final defeat of the rebellion. Having driven the American forces out of Canada and holding strong positions in the major American seaports of New York City and Newport, Rhode Island, the British had options to launch attacks almost anywhere along the eastern seaboard. Two dominant strategies emerged: one designed to draw Washington's army into general battle by threatening the capital city of Philadelphia and the other to renew the operation to seize control of the Hudson River corridor. Burgoyne became the main proponent of the latter strategy. His experience with Carleton the previous year reaffirmed what he had believed from the earliest stages of the war. While serving in Boston in 1775, he wrote in a memo to his commanding officer, General Thomas Gage:

> *I have always thought Hudson's River the most proper part of the whole continent for opening vigorous operations. Because of the course of the river, so beneficial for conveying all the bulky necessities of an army, it is precisely the route that an army ought to take for great purposes of cutting communications between Southern and Northern Provinces, giving confidence to the Indians, and securing a junction with Canadian forces. These purposes effected, and a fleet upon the coast, it is to me morally certain that the forces of New England must be reduced so early in the campaign to give you battle upon your terms, or perish before the end of it for want of necessary supplies.*[5]

John Burgoyne was a well-connected member of England's social elite who, in addition to serving thirty years in the military, was a member of Parliament and a playwright of some renown. Upon his return to England at the end of 1776, he had much to say about Carleton's uninspiring leadership and failure to vigorously prosecute the campaign for control of the Hudson River. He presented his ideas about the strategic value and how a successful operation might be conducted in an essay entitled "Thoughts for Conducting the War from the Side of Canada," which he presented to American Colonial Secretary Lord George Germaine in February 1777.

His proposal called for a two-pronged offensive from Canada supported by a corresponding move up the Hudson River by Howe's army in New York City. He proposed to lead the main column of troops advancing from Canada with the initial objective of securing Lake Champlain by taking Crown Point and Fort Ticonderoga. A smaller force would move down from Canada to the Mohawk River Valley to divert the enemy's attention from the main advance and recruit troops from that area's Loyalist-leaning populace. Burgoyne laid out several alternatives for proceeding after the capture of Fort Ticonderoga, including moving on to the Hudson River to make a junction with Howe at Albany or coordinating with troops in Newport to gain control of the Connecticut River Valley. His broad outlines lacked specifics about the ultimate goals of the campaign, which he left for his superiors to define during the development of the overall plans for 1777.

Germaine supported Burgoyne's proposal and presented it to King George III and his war ministers for their consideration. Howe concurrently devised and proposed his own plans for the upcoming year. On November 30, 1776, he sent two letters to London. The first contained a report on the successful operations in New York, while the second outlined a multipronged offensive that included among its various movements the use of Rhode Island as a base for launching an attack on Boston and the dispatch of a force from New York City to Albany to support an anticipated renewal of Carleton's campaign from Canada. Shortly thereafter, however, Howe became

John Burgoyne (1723–1792) entered the army young and saw service in France and in Canada before the campaign of 1777. His wit and bravery are unquestioned, but he held himself in high esteem and, like most of the British officers, never dreamed that their "superior" force of English gentlemen could be overtaken by the less professional Continental army, made up of "inferior" tradesmen and mechanics. *Lossing*

convinced that his army should focus on the destruction of Washington's army, which he believed might be lured into general battle by threatening the capital city of Philadelphia. On December 20, before his earlier plans reached London, he sent another letter outlining his plans to delay the Rhode Island operation in favor of an overland assault through New Jersey to Philadelphia.

However, Washington's victories at Trenton (December 25–26, 1776) and Princeton (January 3, 1777) soon altered the situation and caused Howe to change his plans again. After the Continental army established winter quarters at Morristown, Washington was in position to harass Howe's flank and supply lines if the British chose to move overland toward Philadelphia. Howe subsequently concluded that the best way to proceed was to sail the bulk of his army to Chesapeake Bay and attack the city from the south. His second in command, Sir Henry Clinton, would be left to hold New York with a small force and with vague orders that authorized him to support any operation from Canada if he were able to do so. Based on the slow progress of the previous year, Howe thought that Carleton would not near Albany until late fall, at which time he hoped to have accomplished his objectives and be able to supply troops from his army.

When the king and his ministers devised the final orders for Burgoyne, they were aware of Howe's intentions to take Philadelphia but did not yet know about the proposed amphibious operation. They ordered Burgoyne to make control of the upper Hudson River Valley his primary objective. Lieutenant Colonel Barry St. Leger was placed in command of the force tasked with creating the diversion Burgoyne had proposed in the Mohawk Valley. When both forces met at Albany and established communications with the command in New York City, Burgoyne was ordered to place himself under Howe's command and support operations in the south. The orders suggested that some form of support from forces on the lower Hudson would be forthcoming, but Howe was already at sea by the time orders reached New York. Clinton had neither the men nor clear orders that would allow him to cooperate with Burgoyne. Burgoyne's ignorance of Howe's plans and his persisting hope of support from the south weighed heavily in his decision-making throughout his campaign and had serious consequences on its prospects for success.

BURGOYNE MOVES SOUTH MAY 6 THROUGH SEPTEMBER 18, 1777

Burgoyne arrived in Quebec on May 6, 1777, and found that Carleton had done much to assemble troops and material at St. Johns on the Richelieu River. Over the course of the following month, the men completed the final preparations. On June 13, the offensive sailed out toward its first destination of Crown Point, New York, near the southern end of Lake Champlain. The right wing of the army under the command of Major General William Phillips consisted of about 3,725 British regulars and 250 Loyalist scouts. About 3,000 German auxiliaries from Braunschweig and Hessen Hanau and 400 Native American warriors from various Iroquois and Algonquin tribes composed the left wing, led by Major General Friedrich Adolph, Baron von Riedesel. The army reserve consisted of about 250 unmounted Braunschweig dragoons under Lieutenant Colonel Frederich Baum. Up to 1,000 noncombatants and

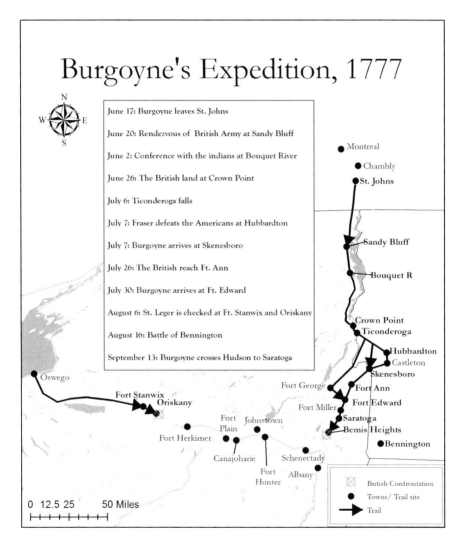

The map tells the story of how Burgoyne's "perfect" plan would have been successful in isolating the New England colonies and cutting off their supply lines, if only unforeseen circumstances had not occurred. *Chaucer/Cooper.*

camp followers, including about 250 women, attended the force. The artillery train consisted of about 138 pieces.

The bulk of the army was to travel by water for much of the trip. Commodore Skeffington Lutwidge assembled dozens of canoes, hundreds of bateaux, nine Royal Navy vessels and twenty-eight gunboats under his command. Overland portions of the campaign required the use of hundreds of carts and draft animals to transport the enormous amount of provisions, baggage, ammunition, equipment and other supplies necessary to support the army. Burgoyne intended to travel by water as far as was practicable since it was the easiest means for transporting the army and its baggage.

After securing an undefended Crown Point, burned by Arnold during his retreat after the Battle of Valcour Island, Burgoyne moved south toward Fort Ticonderoga, where he expected to encounter his first serious opposition. The French initially constructed the fortress, known as the "Gibraltar of America," in 1755–58 to control the strategically important location at the connection between Lake George and Lake Champlain. Benedict Arnold and Ethan Allen had taken the site in one of the few early American successes on May 10, 1775. The sprawling fortress and its outer defensive works required a force of 10,000 to properly man them, but a skeleton force of only about 2,500 under the command of Major General Arthur St. Clair confronted Burgoyne. On July 5, Burgoyne ordered artillery to the commanding summit of Mount Defiance, left unguarded due to St. Clair's limited forces. Under cover of darkness, St. Clair marched the bulk of the forces overland toward Castle Town (now Castleton), Vermont. Colonel Pierce Long was given about 600 men and was charged with evacuating the wounded and sick by boat, along with as much artillery and stores as could be accommodated. Long's objective was Skenesborough, where St. Clair hoped to join him later.

Burgoyne dispatched the army's right-wing Advanced Corps under Brigadier General Simon Fraser and a brigade from Von Riedesel's division to pursue St. Clair's force, which reached Hubbardton, Vermont, on July 6. St. Clair left a small detachment of men under Colonel Seth Warner to cover the army's march and to collect the rear guard, consisting of the Eleventh Massachusetts Regiment under Colonel Ebenezer Francis and stragglers who had become disengaged from their units. Instead of obeying St. Clair's order to move immediately to Castle Town after the forces were joined, Warner and Francis decided to camp for the night at Hubbardton. On the morning of July 7, Fraser surprised them. After the initial shock, the Americans rallied and made a spirited fight, but the two-hour battle ended when a flanking maneuver by Von Riedesel's men forced Warner to order a general retreat. More than half of the about 600 American troops engaged were killed, wounded or captured. British losses came to 35 killed and 148 wounded.

While the Battle of Hubbardton was being waged, Burgoyne's advance guard caught up with Colonel Long at Skenesborough. After a brief skirmish, the Americans retreated south to Fort Ann. Burgoyne detached Lieutenant Colonel John Hill with a force of about 190 men from the Ninth Regiment of Foot to pursue Long, but a nearly impassable road caused delays. He took up a position about one mile from the Americans on the evening of July 7. Soon after reaching Fort Ann, about 400 New York militia troops, whom Schuyler had sent forward under the command of Henry van Rensselaer, reinforced Long. Long decided to attack after gaining intelligence about the relatively small size of Hill's force and nearly succeeded in surrounding the British.

Before the attack could be pressed home, however, an Indian war whoop deceived the Americans into believing that reinforcements had arrived. British captain John Money, who had been sent with a detachment of Indian forces to assist Hill, actually delivered the war cry. When the Indians lagged behind, Money moved forward without them and issued the war whoop as an encouragement to Hill's beleaguered troops that reinforcements were arriving. The Americans heard the cries as well, and the ruse convinced Long to withdraw. He then ordered his troops to move toward Fort Edward. With the loss of Skenesborough and Fort Ann, St. Clair had little choice but to move south to Fort Edward. When he reached the fort on July 12, Schuyler met St. Clair and assumed personal command of the joined American forces.

At Skenesborough, Burgoyne decided on the route he would take to reach the Hudson River. He could either make a retrograde movement to Fort Ticonderoga and continue the operation on water by way of Lake George or march overland to Fort Edward using Wood Creek and an adjacent road. He chose the latter because it eliminated two difficult portages and allowed him to stay in contact with the American main force, which intelligence reports told him was falling back toward Albany. He also considered the effect that the seeming retreat to Fort Ticonderoga would have on the minds of his soldiers and in bolstering the confidence of the Americans, who up to that point had presented little opposition to his advance. The decision meant, however, that Burgoyne had to cut loose a significant number of his boats to transport baggage and supplies over the lake route because the narrow Wood Creek would not allow passage. In the process, his supply line became overextended, and he was forced to depend to a greater degree on foraging in the surrounding countryside to feed his army.

When advised of the British movement on the overland route, Schuyler ordered his engineers to obstruct Burgoyne's advance in the hopes of gaining time to assemble reinforcements for his army. Colonel Thaddeus Kościuszko, a French-trained engineer who later played a critical role in laying out the defensive works at Saratoga, directed hundreds of troops to destroy bridges, fell trees, obstruct Wood Creek and divert its waters to flood the road. Schuyler also ordered local farmers to drive away their cattle to prevent their confiscation by Burgoyne's foraging parties and force the foragers to go farther afield to gather supplies. Schuyler's tactics had the desired effect, as it took Burgoyne twenty-one days to cover the twenty-three miles from Skenesborough to Fort Edward and provided Schuyler with valuable time to gather his forces.

By the time Burgoyne finally reached Fort Edward on August 1, his serious supply problems required him to halt the advance down the Hudson River to address shortages. Two days later, Burgoyne received a letter from Howe regarding his operation against Philadelphia. With little hope of support or resupply from the south, Burgoyne decided to act on a report from Von Riedesel that the Connecticut River Valley held a rich supply of agricultural foodstuffs and livestock, including horses on which he could mount his dragoons. Burgoyne detached a force of about 800 mostly German troops under Lieutenant Colonel Friedrich Baum to cross the Green Mountains to the valley to gather supplies and potentially recruit additional troops. The expedition set out on August 9, and along the way a detachment of British sharpshooters, Loyalists and Native Americans augmented the group, bringing Baum's total strength to about 1,250. Two days later, Burgoyne received intelligence about a lightly guarded Continental supply depot at Bennington, Vermont. He immediately ordered the detachment to march toward that objective because it was much closer to his army.

A force of about 1,500 New Hampshire militia commanded by Brigadier General John Stark met Baum at a crossing of the Walloomsac River four miles northwest of Bennington on August 14. After finding that he was outnumbered, Baum requested reinforcements from Burgoyne and set about constructing defensive works on both sides of the river at the crossing. Burgoyne dispatched Heinrich von Breymann with 660 troops, but heavy rains the following day delayed the advance. Stark launched a full-scale attack on Baum's position on August 16, succeeding in enveloping the force in a three-pronged attack on his center and rear right and left flanks. After a heavy fight and the mortal injury of Baum, the battle wound down by about 4:00 p.m., with the remnants of Baum's forces fleeing back toward Fort Edward. Breymann's relief force met them and pressed on, to be met by Stark, who had been reinforced at about the same time by Seth Warner's command. Again, the Americans prevailed and forced a full retreat. The Battle of Bennington, as it became known, was a resounding victory for the Americans. British losses amounted to some 200 killed and wounded and 700 captured, while Stark's and Warner's casualties were estimated at about 50. The battle also prevented the resupply of Burgoyne's army and, together with the events unfolding almost simultaneously in the Mohawk River Valley, proved a crucial turning point in the fortunes of Burgoyne's campaign.[6]

St. Leger's force, consisting of about 280 British and German soldiers, 800 Iroquois Indians and 470 Loyalists, began its campaign down the Mohawk River Valley from Oswego on Lake Ontario on July 26. Meeting no opposition, St. Leger's column reached Fort Stanwix at Rome, New York, on August 2. It immediately began preparations to lay siege to the fort and its garrison of about 650 New York and Massachusetts troops under the overall command of Colonel Peter Gansevoort. Schuyler had alerted the Tryon County militia under Brigadier General Nicholas Herkimer to expect such a move, and Herkimer was able to quickly assemble a force of about 800 militia and 60 Oneida warriors to come to Gansevoort's aid. St. Leger sent a detachment of about 700 men, mostly Loyalists and Iroquois, under Loyalist Sir John Johnson to meet Herkimer.

Johnson ambushed Herkimer's force at Oriskany on August 6. The Battle of Oriskany was a bloody affair that pitted neighbors fighting on both sides against one another. The Tryon County militia was defeated, with about five hundred killed, wounded or captured. Herkimer was mortally wounded. While the battle took place, however, the Fort Stanwix garrison raided part of St. Leger's camp, capturing or destroying much of its supplies and thereby weakening St. Leger's prospects. On August 12, Schuyler sent forces from the main army to lift the siege at Fort Stanwix. The following day, Schuyler sent Benedict Arnold, who had recently been sent by Congress to take command of the relief force. At German Flats, about thirty miles south of the Oriskany Battlefield, Arnold's men captured a number of Loyalists and convinced one to spread rumors among St. Leger's troops that Arnold was advancing in large numbers. The ruse worked on the Iroquois, who deserted the expedition. At that point, St. Leger decided to abandon his operation and retreat to Canada, foiling another major element of Burgoyne's plans.

The successes against Baum and St. Leger came too late to save Schuyler from Congress's decision to remove him from command of the Northern Department. Congress had become increasingly dissatisfied with Schuyler's performance since the poorly executed operation against

Canada, which Schuyler was supposed to lead until he was forced to withdraw due to poor health. Schuyler's personality and aristocratic Dutch patrician background, combined with a longstanding divide between New York and New England troops, factored into his inability to get along with many of the New Englanders under his command and caused problems in recruiting and commanding troops from those states. On August 10, while in the process of moving the army from Stillwater south to Van Schaick's and Haver (now Peebles) Islands, at the confluence of the Hudson and

General Horatio Gates (1727–1806) was a retired British soldier who had seen service in Europe and in the French and Indian Wars in America. By 1773, he had retired to a plantation in Virginia but offered his services to George Washington at the start of the Revolution. Like Burgoyne, Gates had a high opinion of his own capabilities and thought that he should supplant General Washington as commander. He later sold his plantation, freed his slaves and moved to Manhattan; he served a term in the New York State legislature. *SNHP.*

Mohawk Rivers, Schuyler received a letter from John Hancock, president of Congress, notifying him that he was to be relieved and directing him to report to Washington's headquarters, along with St. Clair, presumably to face court-martial over the loss of Fort Ticonderoga. He remained with the army until August 19, when his longtime rival and former second-in-command Major General Horatio Gates appeared in camp with orders to relieve him.

Upon assuming command, Gates immediately began the process of improving army morale and building up the force to meet Burgoyne. Washington detached Colonel Daniel Morgan's newly formed provisional Rifle Corps, composed of about 500 specially selected marksmen from Pennsylvania, Virginia and Maryland, and ordered 750 men from Israel Putnam's army in the New York highlands to the Northern Department. Arnold, after leaving a garrison of 700 at Fort Stanwix, arrived with an additional 1,200 men.[7]

PREPARATION OF THE AMERICAN DEFENSES ON THE SARATOGA BATTLEFIELD, SEPTEMBER 12–18, 1777

The delay in the British advance provided critical time for the Americans to reorganize and establish a strong defensive position south of Saratoga. By early September, Gates had some 7,500 troops under his command on the west side of the Hudson and another 2,000 to threaten Burgoyne's left flank under Major General Benjamin Lincoln in Vermont. Gates returned north to Stillwater, where he scouted for favorable terrain to establish a fortified defensive position to block Burgoyne's advance. He found such a place three miles north at Bemis Heights and began deploying his army there on September 12.

The American forces controlled Bemis Heights adjacent to the ground that determined the prosecution and outcome of the ensuing battles. The heavily wooded bluff named after Jotham Bemis (or Bemus), a farmer who also kept a tavern below the heights on the Road to Albany, perched above a steep escarpment rising from a narrow defile of cleared flatland between its base and the river. Immediately to the north, a wider area of swampy ground occupied the area within an eastern bend of the river. The Road to Albany, the route that Burgoyne had to travel to maintain contact with the river, ran through the lowlands, fully visible to observation and fire from the heights above it. The combination of the alluvial flats to the immediate north, known as the "Vly" (Dutch for swamp or marsh), and the natural defile created by the near-intersection of the bluffs, road and river severely limited an enemy army's maneuverability and tactical options. (The SNHP trail system crosses the paths of the roads present in 1777, revealing the circulation options available to the troops.)

Gates placed Colonel Thaddeus Kościuszko, engineer, in charge of erecting field fortifications to strengthen the American position. Kościuszko constructed a series of mutually supporting redoubts on the bluff and placed artillery there. More guns were placed in the lowlands between the road and the river where the Americans dug a trench and built breastworks that provided a protected open field of fire on the Road to Albany. If Burgoyne attempted to pass through the gauntlet at the base of the heights, American artillery on the road and the bluff above it could subject the British army to withering enfilade.

Burgoyne's other alternative was to ascend the heights and either bring the Americans to battle or circumvent their position. The area north of the American position consisted of heavy woods interspersed with small farm fields, ravines and streams, while traditional British military tactics favored open ground where they could mass strength in formation

Thaddeus Kościuszko (1746–1817) bears the distinction of being a national hero in Poland, Lithuania, the United States and Belarus. Born in what was then the Polish-Lithuanian Commonwealth, he received a fine military education, spent time in Paris studying engineering and went to America in 1775, eager to help the cause. He was soon accepted into the Continental army as a colonel and named its head engineer. *Lossing.*

and maneuver freely. Gates and Kościuszko recognized, however, that Bemis Heights was vulnerable to attack from higher ground about three-quarters of a mile to the west on the farm belonging to John Neilson. Accordingly, Kościuszko constructed fortifications and placed artillery along the summit of the hill and along the crest of the ravine draining down toward American Creek. His men cut thousands of trees to build fortifications and create clear fields of observation and fire; this would make the position immune to surprise attack. In addition, Kościuszko destroyed bridges over streams and felled trees across the roads leading to the American position to make enemy movements, particularly artillery, more difficult. These batteries and fortifications dictated the tactics of both armies and the course of the ensuing battles.

Gates organized the army into two wings, the left consisting of Morgan's Corps and the brigades of Brigadier Generals Enoch Poor and Ebenezer Learned and the right of the brigades of Brigadier Generals John Patterson, John Nixon and John Glove, under his own command. The bulk of the army defended the heights around John Neilson's farm. Its position resembled an inverted "V," with the western leg beginning south of a road leading west from the Road to Albany to Saratoga Lake and the eastern leg extending southeast along a deeply cut ravine toward Bemis Heights. The apex of the V was just north of the John Neilson House, the only surviving building that was present at the time of the battles.

John Neilson built the house about two years earlier when he moved to the area from his native New Jersey. He enlisted in the Continental army, and his house was vacant when the opposing armies took up their positions. Located on a hill overlooking much of the American lines to the east and west, the house was an obvious choice as quarters for the left wing's general staff. Both Enoch Poor and Benedict Arnold are said to have occupied it during the course of the battles. Smaller bodies of men supported the Bemis Heights redoubts, the entrenchments along the Road to Albany and an outpost west of the Neilson Farm. A skirmishing detachment headed north on the Road to Albany to provide advance warning should Burgoyne choose that route. Gates established his headquarters in Ephraim Woodworth's house on the south side of the road to Saratoga Lake where he could readily communicate with both wings.

THE FIRST BATTLE OF SARATOGA (FREEMAN'S FARM), SEPTEMBER 19, 1777

On September 18, Burgoyne finalized his plans to attack the Americans. He knew of the commanding position that Gates held at Bemis Heights. Tied to the river to float his supplies, Burgoyne had to decide whether to force his way through the strong position or attempt a flanking movement. He decided against a direct assault along the Road to Albany and chose instead to explore the possibilities in the uplands and coordinate an attack on the American army's left wing. Burgoyne devised a three-pronged attack using the available roads leading south and west from Sword's farm toward the American position. He gave Fraser the responsibility for executing the flanking movement by taking about 2,400 men, including his Advanced Corps and most of the Loyalist and Native American troops, three miles on a road leading westward and then south toward the Great Ravine. Breymann's Reserve Corps (about 530 troops) followed as a back-up force.

Burgoyne chose to move with the center column comprised of about 1,700 troops from the British right wing under Brigadier General James Hamilton. This column moved west behind Fraser for a short distance before turning south on a road leading down to the Great Ravine. From there it planned to cross the ravine and take up a position north of John Freeman's farm. Von Riedesel led the left column consisting of about 1,600 mostly German troops on the Road to Albany, bringing the main artillery and guarding supplies and the boats on the river. Upon reaching their designated positions, a prearranged signal of guns would mark the commencement of simultaneous movements against the American camp. With the order of battle set, the operation began in the morning of September 19.

After receiving information from his advance pickets that Burgoyne was on the move, Gates initially thought to await attack from behind his strong entrenchments. Arnold, however, felt that his left flank was vulnerable to the type of move Burgoyne was attempting and requested that he be allowed to send a reconnaissance force to determine Burgoyne's intentions. If, as he feared, they were found to be advancing on his left, Arnold believed it better to check them north of the army's position, where the heavy woods and uneven topography would allow his light infantry to operate more effectively than the British. After gaining Gates's assent, Arnold ordered Morgan's Corps, which consisted of Morgan's rifle battalion and Major Henry Dearborn's light infantry battalion, to move out on the road leading north from Neilson's farm toward Freeman's farm. Morgan positioned his men around Freeman's house and barn located on a hill near the western edge of the farm's clearing.

At about noon, the advance pickets of Hamilton's center column emerged from the woods at the northern end of the Freeman Farm clearing. Morgan's men met them with fire that struck down

Benedict Arnold (1741–1801) achieved great military success in the Continental army, rising to the rank of general, but for a variety of reasons, including feeling insufficiently recognized as a leader, he switched his allegiance to the British side and died in London. *Lossing.*

all of the officers present and most of the troops. Those who survived retreated in disorder into the woods, where Hamilton's main force opened fire, believing them to be Americans. As Morgan's men pursued, advance units of Fraser's corps attacked on their flanks, forcing the Americans to scatter into the woods at the southern end of the farm. Arnold sent three New Hampshire regiments from Poor's Brigade to reinforce Morgan at his position. Hamilton assembled his four regiments at the clearing's northern end.

Hamilton's Sixty-second Regiment moved out across the field to resume the fight at about 3:00 p.m. The Americans attacked on the regiment's front and left flank. Coming on despite the heavy fire, the British attempted a bayonet charge, but the Americans repulsed it and captured two cannons pushed forward in support of the attack. As Poor's men pursued the retreating British, the British rallied and again advanced on the hill, recapturing the cannons and forcing the Americans to pull back. During the battle, Arnold sent forward additional regiments from Poor's Brigade to support Learned's Brigade, which advanced to the left of Poor's and skirmished with Fraser's column positioned on the McBride and Marshall Farms (west and north of Freeman's farm). Hamilton's Ninth Regiment moved to the right to establish contact with Fraser's left, thwarting any potential for Learned to exploit the gap between the two columns, and posted at two cabins (later known as the Canadian Cabins) flanking the road at the eastern end of McBride's farm clearing. In the meantime, Hamilton's Twentieth Regiment entered the woods on the left of the Sixty-second in an attempt to turn Morgan's right flank.

The fighting at Freeman's farm raged back and forth for about three hours as the forces attacked and counterattacked across the open field. In the meantime, Von Riedesel's left column on the Road to Albany made little progress, spending much of the day establishing defensive positions to guard the army supplies under his care and constructing new bridges along the Road to Albany to replace those destroyed by the Americans. With the sounds of battle heard to the west, Von Riedesel dispatched two companies of the regiment and Von Rhetz to a wooded bluff on the south side of the Great Ravine to cover a road that ran west toward Freeman's farm and to be in position to join the battle if necessary.

When Burgoyne recognized that Hamilton's outnumbered forces were on the verge of breaking, he sent orders to Von Riedesel to send reinforcements to fall on the enemy's right flank. At about 5:00 p.m., Von Riedesel led a force consisting of his own regiment, the two detached Von Rhetz companies and two six-pound artillery pieces under Captain Georg Päusch out onto the wooded road leading toward Freeman's farm. Upon reaching the side branch of the ravine bordering the eastern side of the farm, he sent his troops into the ravine on the American's right flank. Päusch's artillery entered the ravine as well, over an intact bridge, and dragged their guns across the flat clearing along the road to the hills on the other side of the field where the Americans were pushing the British line back. With great difficulty, they brought the guns up onto one of the hills. The Twenty-first Regiment joined Von Riedesel in his attempt to force through the ravine on the southern side of the farm. With the arrival of the reinforcements, the British rallied and pushed forward on the American

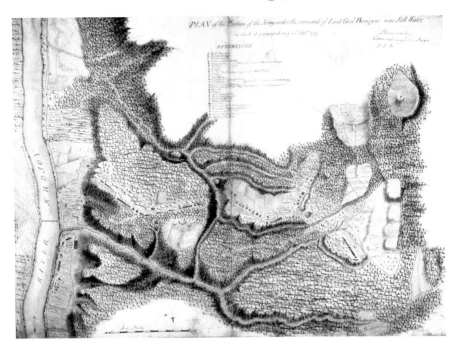

Positions of Burgoyne's army on September 20, 1777 (oriented with south at the top of the map). *SNHP.*

right as night fell, forcing it back for the final time. The engagement ended with nightfall and the American withdrawal from the field.

With the American withdrawal, the British could rightfully claim a tactical victory in the First Battle of Saratoga. The victory, however, did nothing to improve Burgoyne's chances of reaching Albany and came at a significant cost to his dwindling army, which suffered about six hundred men killed, wounded or captured. Gates, who lost about half that number, remained firmly in position to block Burgoyne's path to Albany.

DEFENSIVE INTERVAL BETWEEN THE BATTLES, SEPTEMBER 20 THROUGH OCTOBER 6, 1777

While men on both sides expected the fight to resume the morning of September 20, Burgoyne decided to forestall action to rest his troops. The break also allowed his medical staff to attend to the wounded at his overtaxed field hospital and some regiments to reorganize. Early the following day, he received a letter from Clinton in New York City stating that if Burgoyne thought it would be of help, he was willing to make a push up the lower Hudson. Clinton wrote the letter shortly after learning on September 11 of the defeat at Bennington and the slow progress of Burgoyne's march. He wanted to relieve the pressure on Burgoyne if possible by launching an attack upriver to take Fort Montgomery and other American forts in the area that would draw off troops from Gates's army. With Washington off in Pennsylvania in pursuit of Howe, and expecting his own reinforcement any day, Clinton believed that he could spare two thousand troops to begin the movement "in about 10 days." While hardly a concrete promise of support, the news buoyed Burgoyne, who immediately sent word requesting that Clinton begin his operation as soon as possible. Despite being dangerously low on supplies, Burgoyne determined to dig in and await Clinton's advance.

Later the same day, after hearing a cannonade of celebration from the Americans, Burgoyne learned that Fort Ticonderoga had fallen to the

Situation of Burgoyne's army, west side of the Hudson River, September 20, 1777. *Lossing.*

enemy, and the news reinforced his decision to stay. A force of about 500 men under Colonel John Brown of Major General Benjamin Lincoln's command surprised the British manning the works on September 18 and succeeded in freeing more than 100 American prisoners and capturing more than 250 British and Canadian troops. They also took a large amount of army stores, including arms and provisions. The action proved to Burgoyne that he had little choice but to go forward and that he had to do it soon, as the Americans demonstrated that they were in position to cut both his supply line and his avenue of retreat.[8]

Burgoyne spent the following two weeks strengthening his lines, which stretched in a convex arcing line from the river west to McBride's farm in the northern portion of the Saratoga Battlefield. Natural landscape features separated the army's five distinct units. An encampment of Loyalist and Indian troops—along with the baggage, bateaux and scows, park of artillery, general hospital and supplies—occupied the low plain along the river north of the Great Ravine. Von Riedesel's German troops manned a chain of small posts on the south side of the ravine and also in the lowlands. The bulk of Von Riedesel's left wing of the army and Hamilton's right wing of the army established fortified lines on the plateau above the river on the farm lots leased by John McCarthy and Jeremiah Taylor. The Great Ravine bordered the position on the north, the wood bluff overlooking the river on the east, the Middle Ravine on the south and a deep branch of the Middle Ravine separating the McCarthy and Freeman Farms on the west. Fraser's Advanced Corps occupied Freeman's farm, while Breymann's Reserve Corps occupied the eastern portion of McBride's farm to the north and west.

The men threw up a series of field fortifications along the lines to provide protection in case of attack. The massive construction effort employed more than one thousand men and required the felling of thousands of trees and a significant amount of earth moving. Artillery emplacements on the three hills that rose above the plain to the west guarded the lowland positions. The Great Redoubt located on the southernmost hill just north of the Great Ravine was the most imposing of these. A V-shaped line of abatis protected Hamilton's and Von Riedesel's wings on the plateau.

Fraser's Advanced Corps constructed the strongest position of the entire line around the Freeman Farm buildings, named the Balcarres Redoubt for Major Alexander Lindsay, Sixth Earl of Balcarres, who commanded the Light Infantry Battalion. The oblong fortification with log and earthen walls that ranged from four to fourteen feet in height stretched some five hundred yards on a roughly north–south axis. Eight pieces of artillery supported it. The soldiers constructed a smaller redoubt to the northwest composed of a single line of breastworks about two hundred yards long and seven to eight feet high. It provided cover for Breymann's Reserve Corps and guarded the British extreme right and the road to Quaker Springs. Log and earthen walls fortified the Canadian Cabins, located in the gap between the Balcarres and Breymann Redoubts, along the road leading down to the Great Ravine. In addition to these major structures, the men constructed a number of smaller open-back fortifications throughout the line. Burgoyne also constructed a bridge of bateaux across the river to a *tête-de-pont* (a bridgehead fortification that could be used to protect a bridge from attack or cover a crossing force during retreat) to facilitate foraging and reconnaissance missions and to provide a route for communicating with Clinton.

Gates also made efforts during the lull in fighting to further strengthen his defensive positions on Bemis Heights and continued to receive reinforcements. A growing rift with Arnold became his most significant problem during the interval. Gates had been on good terms with Arnold until recently, when he became increasingly doubtful of his loyalty, suspecting that Arnold was among a group of officers in camp who were openly loyal to his predecessor, General Philip Schuyler. The group spread rumors about Gates's attempts to defame Schuyler, whom he detested, in favor of his assuming command of the Northern Department. For his part, Arnold felt that Gates did not properly support Arnold's attack at Freeman's farm. When Gates reassigned Morgan's Corps to his own command, Arnold became increasingly dissatisfied with his treatment. The rift became serious after Gates failed to mention Arnold in his official report on the First Battle of Saratoga. Arnold, extremely ambitious and jealous of his reputation, took the slight personally and angrily confronted Gates. After being granted a pass to Philadelphia, Arnold refused to leave camp and continued to agitate against Gates among his clique of Schuyler partisans.

By the end of September, Burgoyne's fatigued army was low on provisions. Gates was keenly aware of Burgoyne's situation and determined to do all he could to exacerbate it. On an almost nightly basis, Gates sent skirmishers forward to probe Burgoyne's river defenses and threaten his supply base there. Foraging expeditions met with skirmishes designed to harass and discourage the efforts. These actions further fatigued and demoralized the British army, and an increasing rate of desertion became a serious concern for Burgoyne. On October 3, he announced that rations needed to be cut by one-third but tempered the news by informing the army that help in the form of Clinton's army was on its way.

However, Burgoyne did not have any formal intelligence regarding Clinton's progress. Clinton actually delayed his operation more than a week beyond his proposed start, not getting underway until October 3. He initially headed toward a series of forts on the lower Hudson under the command of Major General Israel Putnam. Putnam had recently sent a good portion of his army to reinforce Washington and was left with a skeleton force of about 1,500 Continental army troops and a number of unreliable militia units. Clinton's force consisted of about 3,000 British Regulars transported on navy vessels.

On October 5, Clinton landed at Verplanck's Point and scattered a force of Americans there. Putnam reacted by moving inland about four miles and ordering reinforcements from Forts Montgomery and Clinton to join him there for an expected attack. Clinton left a force of about one thousand men at Verplanck's to deceive Putnam of his intentions and succeeded in easily taking the undermanned forts. Putnam retreated northward, and Clinton cut the log boom the Americans had erected in the river and easily took Fort Constitution across from West Point on October 7. The next day, he sent word to Burgoyne of the encouraging news that nothing now stood in his way to Albany. By that time, however, the British army had already fought and lost the Second Battle of Saratoga.

On October 4, the day after he cut his men's rations, Burgoyne decided that he could wait no longer for word from Clinton. He called a council of war attended by Generals Phillips, Fraser and Von Riedesel and informed them of his plans to attack the Americans. He proposed to leave eight hundred men to guard the supplies near the river and use the rest of his army to attack Gates's left and rear. The boldness of his plan shocked his subordinates, who advised against it. They argued that a flanking movement would take too much time to execute and be discovered too easily, leaving the force guarding the supplies vulnerable to attack. If the Americans succeeded, the army would lose both its sustenance and escape route. The conference adjourned without reaching a decision.

The next day, Von Riedesel urged Burgoyne to withdraw north of Saratoga to the mouth of the Battenkill, where he could reestablish his supply line with Canada and await Clinton's advance. If Clinton did not arrive, the army could retreat the way it had come. Burgoyne rejected the proposal, believing that the retreat would bring disgrace on the army, and determined to make a last attempt to force his way through the Americans. He revised his plan to make a more conservative attack on Gates through a reconnaissance-in-force that would test Gates's left and forage for supplies along the way. If the reconnaissance found conditions favorable, he would commit the army to a general attack the following day. If the American positions were determined to be too strong, he would acquiesce to Von Riedesel's plan to retreat to Battenkill on the eleventh.

THE SECOND BATTLE OF SARATOGA (BEMIS HEIGHTS), OCTOBER 7, 1777

Burgoyne assembled about 1,700 elite troops from various units of the army to conduct the reconnaissance-in-force, leaving the rest (about 5,400 men) behind to man the defenses. Burgoyne decided to accompany the expedition personally and arranged the troops into three columns under command of his most able officers. Fraser led the right column, which consisted of Balcarres's Light Infantry Battalion, the Twenty-fourth Regiment, and his nephew Captain Alexander Fraser's British Rangers supplemented with a collection of Canadian, Indian and Loyalist troops that would serve as an advance scout unit. The center column under Von Riedesel contained men picked from all the Braunschweig and Hanau units; a detachment of jägers, chasseurs and grenadiers from Breymann's Reserve Corps; and some British troops under Phillips's command. Major John Dyke Acland's British Grenadier Battalion composed the left column. Ten pieces of artillery under the overall command of Major Griffith Williams supported the force.

The operation got underway sometime in the late morning of October 7, with the main force marching south on the Quaker Springs Road, through the abandoned Marshall Farm and out into the open wheat fields of the farms leased by brothers Simeon and Joshua Barber. It quickly drove a small picket of American troops stationed at Simeon Barber's house from the field. At this point, the march halted while foragers cut wheat. Some men attempted to reconnoiter the American lines from the roof of Simeon Barber's house, but tall intervening trees obscured the views. The columns were deployed into a line that stretched about one thousand yards north from the main branch of Mill Creek. Fraser positioned the British light infantry in Joshua Barber's clearing at the base of the wooded hill, with the Twenty-fourth Regiment on its left along a road that led into the woods between the fields. Von Riedesel's men took up a position in Simeon Barber's clearing, with Acland's grenadiers on their left.

Warned that the British were again on the move by the pickets who fled their post on the Barber Farm, Gates sent his aide, Lieutenant Colonel James Wilkinson, to determine the nature of the force. Wilkinson reported that the British were spread out, with their flanks resting on wooded areas that would offer concealment for an attack. With this information, Gates ordered Morgan to prepare to move forward. After consulting further with Wilkinson, Morgan determined that the most vulnerable point was the British right, positioned at the base of the wooded hill on Joshua Barber's farm. He proposed to make a circuit to the left, taking the hill from the west and thereby gaining commanding ground from which his riflemen could enfilade the British ranks. Gates approved the plan and allotted time for the movement in his plans to assail the British left wing simultaneously. He gave that mission to Poor's Brigade, which could take advantage of the concealment offered by the forest cover on Acland's left flank. Poor planned to take his men from the Neilson Farm north along the Quaker Springs Road that led directly to Simeon Barber's farm. Learned followed Poor with the assignment to attack the center to occupy Von Riedesel and prevent him from supporting the columns on the flanks.

Poor's Brigade reached Jesse Chatfield's farm across Mill Creek from Acland's lines at about 3:00 p.m. After learning that his probe had been discovered, Burgoyne decided to abandon plans for further advance on the American left but, believing that he held the high ground and could hold the Americans off, determined to at least allow his foragers to complete their work. He ordered Williams to direct artillery fire on the Americans as a deterrent to their advance. The cannonade had no effect, however, and at about 3:30 p.m., Poor's men emerged from the woods and swept up an open hill, undaunted by a round of small-arms and grape fire that mostly sailed over their heads. Continuing on until they reached close range, the Americans unleashed a heavy volley that felled many of the grenadiers, including Acland, who was shot through both legs and captured. The British retreated in confusion, followed by the Americans, who captured Williams's guns.

Morgan commenced his attack on Fraser on the right side of Burgoyne's lines about the same time that Poor engaged the left. He brought his rifle corps to the hill commanding the British light infantry's position and opened fire. As Simon Fraser attempted to meet the threat by consolidating his flank, Dearborn came up and delivered a devastating close-range volley, followed by a bayonet charge that shattered the formation. The British light infantry fell back toward the woods bordering the Barber Farm and formed a new line across the Quaker Springs Road. With the columns on the right and left dissolving, Learned's Brigade, supported by Brigadier General Abraham Ten Broeck's brigade of New York militia and a regiment from Brigadier General Jonathan Warner's Massachusetts militia, attacked Von Riedesel in the middle. Von Riedesel successfully met the initial attack, forcing the Americans back. While the Americans reformed, Arnold, without orders to do so, appeared on the field to assist in rallying the men and led a fresh assault that forced the Germans to give way. Fraser determined to defend his positions to provide time for Von Riedesel and what was left of Acland's men to organize an orderly retreat but was mortally wounded. The British forces made a general retreat to the Balcarres Redoubt.

By about 5:00 p.m., the remnants of Burgoyne's probing force had taken up positions within the fortified British camp. The probe cost Burgoyne about four hundred casualties and the loss of eight cannons, but his defensive position was strong and the battle was not yet decided. The ensuing fight centered on the main stronghold at the Balcarres Redoubt, attacked first by Poor's men who advanced through the Marshall and Freeman Farms in pursuit of the retreating British. A withering volley met them as they came into the open ground in front of the redoubt and in the face of a superior and entrenched force. Poor decided to pull back to wooded cover.

Meanwhile, Gates sent additional troops to join the action, bringing the total number of the force moving against Burgoyne to about seven thousand men. Following up on their attacks, Morgan and Learned moved on to assault the Breymann Redoubt on the British camp's extreme right. Learned easily swept past the Canadian Cabins, defending the gap between the Breymann and Balcarres Redoubts and invested the now vulnerable southern left of the German position. Morgan hit the Breymann Redoubt from the south and west. During the attack, Arnold, who participated with Poor in his initial assault on the Balcarres Redoubt, rejoined Learned in the attack on the German rear and was wounded in the leg during the fighting. Breymann was killed during the action, which soon turned into a full rout that left the Americans in possession of the German camp and redoubt and fully exposed the British right flank. At that point, the onset of darkness ended the day's fighting. With the superior American force on his flank, Burgoyne ordered a withdrawal during the night to the heights of the Great Redoubt.

BURGOYNE'S RETREAT AND SURRENDER, OCTOBER 8 TO OCTOBER 17, 1777

Burgoyne repositioned his weary and badly injured army the following day near the strongly fortified Great Redoubt. While the Americans advanced into the former British camp and kept up a steady barrage of artillery fire, the British command held a solemn evening burial service for Fraser, who died from his wounds earlier in the day. Burgoyne's options were now limited to either retreat or surrender. He chose to retreat, still retaining the faint hope that Clinton might yet provide relief from the south.

The British began to move northward on the Road to Albany during the afternoon of October 8. Burgoyne had to leave some four hundred wounded at the hospital behind the lines with a letter requesting that Gates provide for their protection. A cold, drenching rain delayed the march as the beaten army struggled to haul its artillery and baggage over the narrow road and along the river by boat. The progress was so slow that the rear guard under Balcarres did not complete its removal until the following day.

Having achieved his initial goal of preventing Burgoyne from reaching Albany, Gates began making plans to capture the entire invading force. He had already done much to position forces in Burgoyne's rear to cut his supply lines and now had the opportunity to use those troops to block his path of retreat. During the week before the second battle, Stark reappeared with his New Hampshire militia to take the small garrison left behind by Burgoyne to guard Fort Edward and began moving down the west side of the river toward Saratoga. A brigade of Vermont militia under Brigadier General Jacob Bailey took up an entrenched position along the road leading north of Fort Edward, and Brigadier General John Fellows took his brigade on the east side of the Hudson to the west end encamped at Saratoga. Some five thousand American troops held positions north and east to prevent Burgoyne's escape as Gates's main force began its pursuit from the south.

Burgoyne arrived at Saratoga on October 9 and found his way north and east blocked. He moved his army to the heights on the west side of the village and spent that evening at Philip Schuyler's country manor, while his engineers began throwing up a hasty but well-placed system of field fortifications in the hills above. The high plateau, later referred to as the "Heights of Saratoga," overlooked the floodplains and confluence of Fish Creek and the Hudson River. Burgoyne passed the site on his way south and knew of its advantages as a defensive position. His men constructed an earthen redoubt along the brow of the hill, encompassing an area of about one hundred acres.

Burgoyne posted most of his British troops and remaining Loyalists on the southern part of the heights north of Fish Creek within the area presently covered by the Victory Woods and Saratoga Monument units of the SNHP. He positioned Von Riedesel's troops to the northeast with the Reserve Corps and the Canadians in the gap between the two wings of the army. The artillery park occupied a rise on the flats east and a little south of the German main body. The position provided Burgoyne with the high ground and had the advantage of commanding an opening that offered a clear field of fire and favorable terrain for the close-order tactics of regular troops.

Gates's advance forces reached the outskirts of Saratoga Village on the morning of October 10. After receiving word of the American approach, Burgoyne ordered Schuyler's house and all outbuildings burned to prevent their use as cover for American operations and moved to the heights. When the Americans reached Schuyler's estate, Colonel Ebenezer Stevens, commander of the artillery, placed his cannons on the flats of the Fish Kill and effectively destroyed Burgoyne's flotilla and the provisions they contained. The following day, thinking that Burgoyne would continue his retreat, Gates ordered an attack on what he thought would be the British rear guard. Instead, the American force faced one of the strongest points on the British entrenched line. A British deserter saved them from a potentially serious reverse by providing information about Burgoyne's entrenched position. Gates averted disaster by calling the troops back before they engaged. Burgoyne later described the lost opportunity to exploit an American mistake as "one of the most adverse strokes of fortune in the whole campaign."

After the aborted attack, Gates determined not to test the strong British lines with a full frontal assault, preferring to complete the envelopment of the position and lay siege. Without resupply, the British could not hold out for long. He completed his movements on October 12 with his army to the south, Morgan on the west, Stark on the north and Fellows to the east. That same day Burgoyne called a council of war to discuss options with his general staff. They faced a critical situation with the army dangerously low on rations and the men exposed without shelter to continuous American artillery bombardment.

Burgoyne outlined five alternatives for his generals to consider, including staying in place and awaiting attack, conducting an attack of their own, retreating with the artillery and baggage, retreating at night without the artillery and baggage or marching rapidly to Albany should the enemy leave its rear open in its shift to the left. He did not yet place surrender on the table. Von Riedesel argued successfully for a rapid retreat at night without the baggage and artillery, but a reconnaissance conducted that day revealed that the American forces to the north and east would discern the movement quickly and prevent its success.

On October 13, Burgoyne again called his staff together for the purpose of gaining consensus on his decision to seek honorable terms for capitulation. Before the meeting, he drafted the articles of a treaty, and he received unanimous support for its terms among the officers. The following day, Burgoyne sent a commission led by his adjutant general, Lieutenant Colonel Robert Kingston, to Gates's headquarters under a flag of truce to begin the negotiations. During the discussion, Gates presented Kingston with his terms, which called for the unconditional surrender of the British army. Despite his desperate situation, Burgoyne was unwilling to surrender under such terms.

To the surprise of the British, Gates soon largely accepted Burgoyne's terms on the condition that the surrender be accomplished by two o'clock on the afternoon of October 15. Burgoyne became suspicious over the imposed deadline, taking it to mean that Gates might be anxious about the impending arrival of Clinton, and decided to prolong the negotiations to buy time. He instructed his commissioners to stall, and they conducted protracted negotiations throughout the following day. Finally, at about eleven o'clock that evening, the commissioners agreed to the terms of the articles of convention that would surrender Burgoyne's army.

During the evening of October 15, Burgoyne received his first knowledge of Clinton's whereabouts when a Loyalist brought word that the advance of the force making its way up the Hudson had reached Esopus, about forty-five miles south of Albany, the week before. Burgoyne called yet another council of war and asked his generals' opinion about whether they thought it honorable to break the articles of convention and, if so, whether they thought the proximity of Clinton's forces improved their situation. A majority of the officers answered no to both questions. Burgoyne, however, continued to hold out hope and sought to delay the negotiations by claiming that they

FAC-SIMILE OF THE SIGNATURES OF BURGOYNE AND GATES
TO THE "CONVENTION."

The signatures of John Burgoyne and Horatio Gates on October 15, 1777, made the Articles of Convention official; it specified that the British troops would be sent back to England, on their word (parole) that they would not fight again in that conflict. All that remained was the formal surrender, two days later. *Lossing* were obtained under false pretense. In an effort to buy time to see what might come of Clinton's advance, he wrote to Gates to request an inspection of his lines to see if a rumored detachment of part of his force to meet Clinton had weakened his position. Gates rejected the request and wrote back that he expected an immediate and decisive decision. With all options exhausted, the British commander signed what was then titled the "Convention of Saratoga" on October 16.

On October 17, Burgoyne and his general staff proceeded to Gates's camp, where the British commander surrendered his sword to the victorious general. In a generous act, Gates returned the sword and invited Burgoyne and his officers to dinner. The British army marched to the Field of Grounded Arms at the site of the former Fort Hardy on the north side of Fish Creek, where it empties into the Hudson River, and piled their weapons. That evening, the defeated British army began a long march to Cambridge, Massachusetts, to be held there until arrangements

Nearly six thousand British troops were forced to lay down their weapons in the field around the ruins of old Fort Hardy. Their dignity was preserved by the privilege of "honors of war"—that is, they were allowed to march out with their unit banners flying. *Lossing.*

John Trumbull's 1821 painting of the surrender found in the U.S. Capitol Rotunda. *SNHP.*

for exchange could be made. Burgoyne was paroled and returned to England in 1778, and many of the officers were exchanged. The rank-and-file troops, however, remained in captivity for the remainder of the war in various prison camps throughout the United States. Following their release, many of the men chose to remain in America.

For the Americans, it was also a time of decision. The destinies of farmers Freeman and Neilson were opposite. Freeman chose to join the British when they arrived in the Saratoga area and left all behind, settling in Canada. Neilson resumed farming, his family prosperous for generations plowing the ground where heated battle had taken place.

EFFECT OF THE SURRENDER AT SARATOGA ON THE AMERICAN REVOLUTION

The battles of Saratoga were pivotal turning points in the American struggle to gain its independence from Great Britain during the Revolutionary War. They represented the culmination of British general John Burgoyne's nearly successful Northern Campaign, which was devised to cut direct communication between New England, considered the hotbed of revolutionary sentiment, and the states to the south. The American victory at Saratoga proved that the Continental army had developed into a formidable fighting force capable of defeating a British army in general battle. It revived the flagging hopes of the supporters of the Revolution and provided the convincing proof that France needed to decide early the following year to enter the war on the side of the United States. French military and provisioning assistance helped to tip the balance in favor of the Americans, leading to their final victory at Yorktown, Virginia, in 1781 and to the establishment of the United States as a free and independent nation.[9]

EFFECTS OF THE VICTORY AT SARATOGA: CREASY

A clear statement of the impact was made by British historian Sir Edward Creasy in his classic work *Fifteen Decisive Battles of the World, from Marathon to Waterloo* (1851):

> *Gates, after the victory, immediately despatched Colonel Wilkinson to carry the happy tidings to Congress. On being introduced into the hall, he said: "The whole British army has laid down its arms at Saratoga; our own, full of vigor and courage, expect your order. It is for your wisdom to decide where the country may still have need for their service." Honors and rewards were liberally voted by the Congress to their conquering general and his men; "and it would be difficult" (says the Italian historian) "to describe the transports of joy which the news of this event excited among the Americans. They began to flatter themselves with a still more happy future. No one any longer felt any doubt about their achieving their independence. All hoped, and with good reason, that a success of this importance would at length determine France, and the other European powers that waited for her example, to declare themselves in favor of America. There could no longer be any question respecting the future, since there was no longer the risk of espousing the cause of a people too feeble to defend themselves.*

The truth of this was soon displayed in the conduct of France. When the news arrived at Paris of the capture of Ticonderoga, and of the victorious march of Burgoyne towards Albany, events which seemed decisive in favor of the English, instructions had been immediately despatched to Nantes, and the other ports of the kingdom, that no American privateers should be suffered to enter them, except from indispensable necessity, as to repair their vessels, to obtain provisions, or to escape the perils of the sea. The American commissioners at Paris, in their disgust and despair, had almost broken off all negotiations with the French government; and they even endeavored to open communications with the British ministry. But the British government, elated with the first successes of Burgoyne, refused to listen to any overtures for accommodation. But when the news of Saratoga reached Paris, the whole scene was changed.

Franklin and his brother commissioners found all their difficulties with the French government vanish. The time seemed to have arrived for the House of Bourbon to take a full revenge for all its humiliations and losses in previous wars. In December a treaty was arranged, and formally signed in the February following, by which France acknowledged the Independent United States of America. This was, of course, tantamount to a declaration of war with England. Spain soon followed France; and before long Holland took the same course. Largely aided by French fleets and troops, the Americans vigorously maintained the war against the armies which England, in spite of her European foes, continued to send across the Atlantic. But the struggle was too unequal to be maintained by this country for many years; and when the treaties of 1783 restored peace to the world, the independence of the United States was reluctantly recognized by their ancient parent and recent enemy, England.

All the physical essentials for national strength are undeniably to be found in the geographical position and amplitude of territory which the United States possess: in their almost inexhaustible tracts of fertile but hitherto untouched soil; in their stately forests, in their mountain-chains and their rivers, their beds of coal, and stores of metallic wealth; in their extensive seaboard along the waters of two oceans, and in their already numerous and rapidly increasing population. And when we examine the character of this population, no one can look on the fearless energy, the sturdy determination, the aptitude for local self-government, the versatile alacrity, and the unresting spirit of enterprise which characterize the Anglo-Americans without feeling that he here beholds the true moral elements of progressive might.

"Even of those great conflicts, in which hundreds of thousands have been engaged and tens of thousands have fallen, none has been more fruitful of results than this surrender of thirty-five hundred fighting men at Saratoga. It not merely changed the relations of England and the feelings of Europe towards these insurgent colonies, but it has modified, for all time to come, the connection between every colony and every parent state." —Lord Mahon

Chapter 3

Memory and Monuments

While the young American republic wrestled with the formalities of treaties ending the Revolutionary War in 1783, General George Washington paid a visit to his old friend, General Philip Schuyler, at his summer home in Saratoga. A high priority was a guided tour of the battlefield area just south of Schuyler's estate. Future presidents Thomas Jefferson and James Madison followed him on a northern, mostly recreational, tour in late spring of 1791. Local farmers were sometimes available to hop on board the carriages of visitors from Albany or Saratoga Springs to provide guided tours of the area, as did Ezra Buel, a veteran of the battles. But while the importance of this place of victory remained prominent in the minds of officials and local residents, recognition of the significance of Saratoga and other sites began to wane in the public's attention over the following decades.

At the same time, esteem for George Washington's personal, military and civic virtues began to elevate his reputation to mythic status. A grand memorial proposed for the District of Columbia soon after his death in 1799 was not organized until 1832; decades of discussion about the nature of memorials ensued before the Washington Monument was finally opened to the public in 1888. At Saratoga, as well, ideas about tangible commemorations took a long time to be realized.

The end of the War of 1812 had closed the chapter on America's break with Great Britain, allowing the young country to look back on its

One of the military items surrendered at Saratoga was a regimental drum, which made its way into the collection of the museum at West Point. *WPM.*

colonial days and Founding Fathers with fondness and admiration. States, cities and villages began observing the Fourth of July as Independence Day even during the Revolutionary War, with national festivities observed on the fiftieth anniversary of the ratification of the Declaration of Independence in 1826. Annual commemorations recalled this event to public memory through planned and spontaneous events and through permanent memorial structures such as plaques or monuments, all meant to be visible reminders of how the United States came to be and the values shared by its citizens.

Thoughtful leaders sought to celebrate the enduring American virtues of courage, honor, self-sufficiency and self-determination, even as the physical evidence of the past began to disappear. The Saratoga Battlefield was reverting to pastures, farms, hills and deeply cut ravines, the great earthworks of opposing armies sinking back into the soil. Only a few suggested that it should be viewed as hallowed ground.

BUILDING MEMORIALS

Among those who viewed the site of the first American victory over the British army as worthy of permanent recognition was a group of patriotic gentlemen who met for a celebratory banquet at the Schuyler House in Schuylerville on October 17, 1856. They founded the Saratoga Monument Association (SMA) that night, with this sentiment, as recorded by SMA member William L. Stone:

The battles of Bemis Heights and of Saratoga (Stillwater), and the surrender of Lieutenant-General John Burgoyne, on the 17th of October, 1777, formed a niche in the Temple of Liberty which Patriotism will one day fill with an appropriate monument.[10]

According to historian Stone, the trustees chose a site for the Saratoga Monument on a high hill with a fine view of the surrounding landscape in Victory Mills at the border of the village of Schuylerville, where the British army had camped the night before its surrender. However, the outbreak of the Civil War in 1861 "cast such a gloom over the whole country and taxed the patriotic energies of the people to such an extent, that the movement to build the monument was suspended up to the year 1872," requiring the SMA to reorganize to regain momentum. After the New York legislature revised the SMA charter, the organization was revived with an expanded roster of distinguished officers and twenty-seven eminent trustees.

As the centennial of the country's birth approached, and with the Civil War a recent memory, local, state and national organizations awoke to the need to express again those ideals of resisting tyranny and preserving unity by appealing to deeply patriotic ideals of freedom and equality. Patriotic embers were fanned to a flame culminating in the Centennial Exposition at Philadelphia, attended by about 1 million visitors during the seven months it was open in 1876.

The SMA, frustrated in its attempts to raise funds from Congress and New York State following the economic depression of 1873, collected enough money from private sources to dedicate the monument's base in time for the centennial of Burgoyne's surrender, October 17, 1877. A "splendid civic, masonic and military procession" stretching for two miles arrived at the hilltop, where forty thousand people took part in the ceremonies. Among the invited officials were the architect, J.C. Markham, and the grand master of the New York State Masonic Order, who "in due and ancient form" laid the 10-foot-square, 2-foot-high cornerstone of Cape Cod granite donated by Booth Brothers stonemasons. The granite slabs were shipped from New York City in a canal boat up the Hudson River and Champlain Canal to Schuylerville. The monument, originally designed to be 80 feet square at the base and 230 feet high, had to be scaled down, in light of funds available, to 38 feet square at

In a niche inside the Saratoga Monument's cornerstone were placed copies of speeches and histories of the Battlefield, the Monument Association and the Revolutionary War; a Bible; coins of 1777 and 1877; flags; and a variety of contemporary newspapers. *SSHM.*

the base and 154½ feet high. Ultimately, most of the original design elements were included.

Jared Clark Markham (1816–1905), the architect of the Saratoga Monument, appears to have been chosen, without competition, because he was an acquaintance of William L. Stone, chairman of the Committee on Design. Markham agreed to accept the commission without the prospect of immediate payment, which likely also contributed to his selection by the financially strapped organization. He never was fully compensated for his design work on the structure or its adornments.

The Saratoga Monument Association enlisted newspaper editors, including Adolph Ochs of the *New York Times*, eminent politicians and citizens of several other states in raising interest and funds from private sources. Bowing to the argument that such monuments were of national,

Above: The Saratoga Monument was finally dedicated in 1912, with New York State governor Dix leading off the orations. *SSHM.*

Right: Bronze plaques designed by architect Markham line the walls of the first floor inside the monument, representative of late nineteenth-century attitudes. This panel depicts the "idle, extravagant British ladies," in contrast to the "industrious, self-denying and frugal American women of 1776" portrayed nearby. *SSHM.*

The statue of General Philip Schuyler, sculpted by Alexander Doyle, is positioned to look out at his (former) vast estate and the canal he envisioned. Colonel Daniel Morgan (not pictured), sculpted by William R. O'Donovan, looks west to the area where his regiment of riflemen held the British army at siege. General Horatio Gates (not pictured), sculpted by George Bissell, looks north, where the British army had marched from Canada to its ultimate defeat at Saratoga. The south niche, reserved for General Benedict Arnold, is empty to symbolize his subsequent treason. *SSHM.*

not just local, importance, eventually Congress and the New York State legislature freed up enough money to complete the structure. The capstone was set in place in 1882, and the statuary, bronze plaques and interior tile work were completed in 1887. The SMA, out of money, disbanded and deeded the monument and its surrounding few acres to New York State. The formal dedication did not occur until the 135th anniversary of the surrender in 1912, fifty-six years after the original proposal.

Even before patriot, educator and civic mover Ellen Hardin Walworth of Saratoga Springs became the first woman to join the SMA Board in 1880, she wrote a guide to the battlefield and chaired the SMA's Committee on Tablets to erect markers and memorials to help visitors learn of its significance in time for the centennial observances. Many of these tall, square granite markers are still in place, marking such sites as

Ellen Hardin Walworth's interest in patriotic causes was helped, in part, by the tradition of her great-grandfather, who had fought at Saratoga with Morgan's troops. As a founder of the national Daughters of the American Revolution and of the Saratoga Chapter of the DAR, she was able to express her patriotism usefully. *SSHM.*

To replace a set of wooden directional signs of the 1880s, DAR members later had granite signposts erected near Saratoga Lake, starting in 1904. *Libby Holmes.*

the fall of British general Fraser and the Bemis Tavern, which may have served as General Lincoln's headquarters. A few, funded by descendants, were family memorials.

It was the same Ellen Hardin Walworth who joined with three other women in 1890 to found the Daughters of the American Revolution (DAR) "to restore to love of country a sense of sober earnestness and civic responsibility." A stated goal was to rescue American patriotism from the traditional Fourth of July "bombast and folly." The DAR put emphasis on preserving the historical record. Mrs. Walworth also spurred the founding of the National Archives and founded the Saratoga chapter of the DAR in 1894. For many years, members celebrated the "Victory of 1777" with luncheons and picnics on the battlefield's grounds. In

The DAR pavilion, designed by architect Stanton P. Lee, was dedicated in 1925 and joined nearby in 1931 by a monument to the "Unknown American Dead," designed by Brython Jones in the Art Deco style. To fund the monument, the organization solicited donations of $0.30 from the entire DAR membership and succeeded in raising a total of $11,000.00 over a period of two years. The pavilion and a memorial grove of trees were removed by the National Park Service thirty-five years later, but the monument remains an important feature. *SSHM.*

The memorial reads: "Thaddeus Kosciuszko 1746–1817. In memory of the noble son of Poland, Brigadier General Thaddeus Kosciuszko, military engineer, soldier of the War of Independence, who under the command of General Gates selected and fortified these fields for the great battle of Saratoga which the invader was vanquished and American freedom assured. Erected by his compatriots, AD 1936." *SSHM.*

1925, the DAR erected a colonial-style pavilion as a shelter for meetings and public events.[11]

Other families and civic groups had their own monuments installed, including one by the Rockefeller Family Association in 1932 to honor nine ancestors who served at Saratoga and one to honor Thaddeus Kościuszko, dedicated in 1936 by the Polish-American Congress, which holds annual ceremonies here.

BENEDICT ARNOLD: AN INCONVENIENT HERO

Recognizing the heroic actions of General Benedict Arnold at Saratoga presents a classic problem. How do you praise genuine valor in light of later treason? Arnold had a clear record of valiant action for the Patriot cause in actions at Quebec, Ticonderoga, Valcour, Danbury and Saratoga. Though crippled by multiple wounds to his left leg (hence the

Designed by George Bissell, the "boot" monument was placed by the SMA in 1887 to commemorate the role of Benedict Arnold in the battles of Saratoga and is the only monument in the Saratoga Battlefield site that does not contain the name of the person being honored. Originally located at the crest of the hill at the Breymann Redoubt site, it was moved to its current site at Tour Stop 7 in 1975. *SSHM.*

boot symbol), suffered in various skirmishes, he maintained his military capacities, even as he switched his allegiance to the British side in 1780. By the mid-nineteenth century, the name of Benedict Arnold was a synonym for traitor; he was portrayed as the mythic sum of all ill repute, the polar opposite of the "sainted" George Washington.

The truth is, of course, much more complex than that black-and-white picture. The problem of how to recognize his contributions to the American cause at Saratoga was resolved by the Boot Memorial, donated in 1887 by SMA member Civil War general John Watts De Peyster. Without mentioning Arnold's name, its inscription reads: "In memory of the most brilliant soldier of the Continental army, who was desperately wounded on this spot, winning for his countrymen the decisive battle of the American Revolution, and for himself the rank of Major General." At the Saratoga Monument, where three niches are occupied by statues of Generals Gates and Schuyler and Colonel Morgan, the fourth, General Arnold's place, is empty.

Building Memory through Events

As mentioned earlier, not all of the commemorations were physical structures. Some were cultural events on small and large scales, but none was as grand as the Saratoga Pageant of 1927. With strong support from the Empire State chapter of the Sons of the American Revolution (SAR), the Rochester chapter of the SAR and two local Rotary Clubs, the Saratoga Battlefield Association (SBA) was chartered in 1923 to preserve the historic areas from development and to protect them for the future. Among the first acts of the SBA was the formation of a committee to plan how the organization would observe the 150th anniversary of the victory at Saratoga, four years hence.

The first decades of the twentieth century saw a growing American passion for historical pageantry, lavishly produced theatrical entertainments that celebrated local and national history in music, dialogue and dance. Professional pageant masters traveled to different sites, primarily in the northeastern United States, engaging the services of local musicians and historians to produce a script that incorporated Indian lore, European exploration, colonial vignettes, religious and military scenes and local immigration and settlement stories. Typically, hundreds if not thousands of people took part, blending a sense of common purpose with growing pride in local history, a unifying bond both for participants and audience members.

As a warm-up for the Surrender Sesquicentennial, a four-day extravaganza celebrated the nation's 150th birthday in 1926 with bands, orations, plays and reenactments in Fort Hardy Park in Schuylerville. Hundreds of schoolchildren performed in parades, choirs, orchestras, dances and skits, under the watchful eye of Miss M. Dorabelle Strong. The evening of July 7 ended with a colonial parade and dancing in the park "with room for 5000 couples."[12]

For the Surrender observances on October 8, 1927, even more spectacular plans involved honorary and working committees from thirteen New York counties, the governors of New York and neighboring states, the Conservation Commission, the State Education Department and the crucial participation of the New York National Guard. The day began with a 150-gun salute at the battlefield, continued with walking tours guided by Sons of the Revolution in Continental uniform, embraced

Above: By various counts, as many as 160,000 people converged on the Saratoga Battlefield to view the spectacular pageant staged with a literal "cast of thousands" for the 150th anniversary of Burgoyne's surrender, the "turning point" of the Revolutionary War. *SNHP.*

Left: The State of New Hampshire, the only one of the thirteen original states that responded to an invitation to contribute a monument, dedicated a memorial during the 1927 sesquicentennial observances to honor its troops under General Enoch Poor and the colonels of his three regiments. *SSHM.*

the dedication of the monument by the State of New Hampshire and dedicated the grounds as a public battlefield park, with appropriate blessings, speeches and martial music.

For the afternoon's entertainment and edification, Percy Jewett Burrell (1877–1964) of Boston, the "king" of pageant masters, adapted, produced and directed a grand spectacle titled *Why America Is Free*. The events were planned and rehearsed in every detail, with military precision in logistics and timing. A special temporary switchboard and telephone service was installed at the battlefield by the National Guard. In all, 6,500 participants enacted the history of the battlefield, starting at 2:00 p.m. with a dance depicting the glacial formation of the Hudson River Valley, through the dramatization of the battles and the surrender of General Burgoyne. The pageant ended precisely at 5:00 p.m. with "The Star-Spangled Banner," accompanied by a parade of angels of victory, foreign dignitaries, messengers of peace, the DAR and equestrian units of the National Guard. The evening was capped by a VIP banquet in Victory Mills, with Governor Alfred E. Smith as master of ceremonies and speeches carried to a wide audience by radio station WGY, a pioneer in broadcasting from remote sites.[13]

As the battlefield became an official park under New York State's care, the people and events commemorated at Saratoga were now described in

In the sesquicentennial celebration, Lieutenant General John Burgoyne (portrayed by Brigadier General Ransom H. Gillett, commander, NYSNG 53rd Infantry Brigade), General Gates (portrayed by Lieutenant Colonel Bernard W. Kearney, commander, 105th Infantry) and General Schuyler (portrayed by Major Ogden A. Ross) are all looking somewhat jollier than would have the original cast. *SSHM.*

their regional and national context. The Saratoga Monument was seen to celebrate not just Burgoyne's surrender but also the necessary prior military actions at Bennington and Oriskany. The Saratoga Battlefield was on its way to becoming a nationally recognized, sacred landscape, as well as a collective memory of sacrifice and valor.

By 1938, when the Saratoga Battlefield became an official national park, more than twenty monuments, memorials and historical signs dotted the landscape between Stillwater and Schuylerville. The park was already established as a memorial ground. Today, commemorative practices and observances continue via reenactments, interpretive programs and festivities, as described in the sixth chapter.

As a final salute to the commemorative movement, it is appropriate to note the role played in the 1970s and '80s by Chatham Artillery punch, an authentic and potent eighteenth-century recipe of assorted liquors and fruits, mixed and fermented over several months' time. The grown children of a former park historian now recall waking up on the morning of July 5 to find the lawn of the Schuyler House decorated by the recumbent forms of celebrants felled the night before in their historically accurate, enthusiastic and patriotic quaffing of multiple toasts to the cause of liberty.[14] This tradition, sadly, is no longer observed in quite the same way.

Chapter 4

Becoming a National Park

After the Saratoga Monument Association had erected the Saratoga Monument in Victory and installed numerous memorials in the battlefield area, the transition of the battlefield sites from private farms to public parkland continued in earnest when the Saratoga Battlefield Association (SBA) was formed in 1923. The SBA began acquiring land that later became the basis for the park, first buying, with the help of *New York Times* publisher Adolph Ochs, the Sarle and Freeman Farms.

Fervent requests for funding the Saratoga project were shot down, both in Congress and in the New York State legislature, with bills introduced and hopes raised, then dashed when the proposals were either tabled or vetoed. State Assemblyman Burton D. Esmond (1922–33), a lawyer from Ballston Spa, New York, took the appeal to area Rotary Clubs, where he found the right man at the right time.

George O. Slingerland was a self-described "battlefield fanatic." He was not only the president of the Mechanicville Rotary Club but also the mayor of that city just south of the battlefield, and he had a summer home at Bemis Heights at the battlefield's edge. Slingerland took up the challenge by rallying area Rotarians, veterans' groups and civic organizations to raise money and apply political pressure on state legislators. He built a constituency strong enough to move the project to reality. Appointed to the Temporary Advisory Board on Battlefields and Historic Sites during the transition to New York State's ownership, Slingerland became the Battlefield's first superintendent.

A key moment in the sesquicentennial celebrations of 1927 was the official assumption of the Battlefield by the State of New York, which had finally released some funds to purchase land and add "improvements and rehabilitation."[15]

During the state's management period, the Conservation Commission, which oversaw New York State parks and forestland, planted grass to create a more open and park-like setting and demolished numerous post– Revolutionary War features in the area, including barns, stone walls, houses and hedgerows. To increase public use of the parkland, the state constructed three miles of gravel roads and provided visitor facilities such as parking areas, restrooms and picnic tables. In keeping with prevailing ideas of presenting history, the state renovated the Neilson House and built a replica stone powder house, a "period house" to portray General Arnold's headquarters and a blockhouse constructed of materials from

Following the contemporary example of reconstruction and replication at Williamsburg, New York State built structures that might have been found near the Neilson Farm on the Battlefield. The "period house" and replica powder house were removed as unauthentic in the early 1940s; the blockhouse was moved in 1975 to Stillwater, where it serves as a local museum and visitor center in the summer. *SSHM.*

earlier structures. The replica blockhouse served as the park's first visitor center, although the collections of artifacts found on the battlefield outgrew their space by 1931and were displayed at the Colonial Room of the Athenaeum (library) in Saratoga Springs.

In the optimism and booming economy that followed the First World War, the 1920s saw an increase in patriotism, prosperity and mobility. Many families now had cars, which they used in increasing numbers to visit national parks and historic sites. Under Superintendent Slingerland, the Saratoga Battlefield geared up to receive visitors and began a concerted effort to educate children and adults about why this place was so significant. Until his death in 1932, Slingerland worked to increase the Park's acreage, to enhance it as a commemorative landscape and to improve visitors' understanding. A memorial tablet, originally dedicated in 1938 by local Rotary Clubs, was moved to the wall at the foot of the path to the Visitor Center in 1962. It extols George Slingerland, whose "vision, patriotism and untiring efforts were largely responsible for the acquisition, development and preservation of the Saratoga Battlefield." He paved the way for Saratoga Battlefield to become a national historical park.

Nationally, the first movements to preserve battlefields focused on sites of the Civil War, more recent in memory. In 1890, the first four national military parks were created under the management of the War Department. Proponents of other military sites in many different states petitioned for similar status. By 1926, the clamor was sufficient for Congress to authorize the Army War College to conduct a study that would establish a priority list for creating national military parks and memorials. Saratoga Battlefield emerged as one of the top five for its outstanding military and historical significance.

FRANKLIN ROOSEVELT TAKES AN INTEREST

Saratoga was fortunate to have another champion with even greater clout to get things done. As governor of New York (1929–32), Franklin D. Roosevelt expressed great interest in the development of the Saratoga Battlefield and, from the first, supported it becoming a federal property. On October 8, 1929, he was the featured speaker at an annual Rotary observance at the Battlefield. In a cold wind and spitting snow, Roosevelt unleashed his best rhetoric: "[Saratoga was] the scene of much more than a battle. It was a scene of the birth of American independence in fact, just as surely as the Declaration of Independence was the birth in theory. The field, therefore, is a shrine." He urged that "state and nation should work hand in hand in keeping the memory of freedom and liberty alive here."[16]

The newspaper account continued:

> *Halfway through his address, Mrs. Howard H. Hall, in full Colonial Dame regalia, tiptoed forward and besought the governor to put on his hat to avoid a cold.*
>
> *"I was born without a hat," said the Governor, smiling.*
>
> *"But you mustn't take chances with your health," said Mrs. Hall, also smiling.*
>
> *The Governor covered his head. "I always obey a colonial dame," he explained.*

Franklin Roosevelt, after speaking eloquently to one thousand Rotarians and their guests, took shelter from a cold, biting wind to have tea in the "period house" with members of the Colonial Dames, suitably attired for the occasion. *SNHP.*

Less than two weeks later, the stock market crash of 1929 plunged the country into economic crisis. As governor, Roosevelt created a temporary relief act that put ten thousand men to work on forestry projects around the state. Shortly after his inauguration in 1933, President Roosevelt signed legislation creating the Civilian Conservation Corps, one of the most famous New Deal programs. The CCC, also known as Roosevelt's Tree Army, would ultimately give work, hope and self-respect to 3 million American men.

Saratoga Battlefield hosted a camp, one of 4,500 that operated nationally during the nine CCC years, and one of 600 overseen by the National Park Service. Here 150 men were housed in nearby Stillwater and worked on projects ranging from reforestation to stabilizing the banks of streams. An incident related by Andrew Tweedie, CCC camp director, reveals the depth of Roosevelt's involvement in the development of the battlefield.

By 1940, the new National Historical Park was still using the blockhouse and had no building large enough to host major exhibits and programs.

Civilian Conservation Corps members labor to remove a cement foundation from the historic battlefield. The Saratoga Battlefield CCC camp operated in 1939 and 1940, helping to restore the landscape to its 1777 appearance. *SNHP.*

A telegram was delivered to Park Superintendent Al Kress on the morning of October 7 announcing that President Franklin D. Roosevelt, who maintained a high degree of interest in the Saratoga Battlefield, was coming to visit the proposed sites for a new visitor center at one o'clock that afternoon.

Two sites were accessible, but the third, a clearing on Murphy's Hill (now called Fraser's Hill), had no way for a car to carry the paraplegic president to the top of the steep, wooded hill. The solution? Mobilize the CCC campers to build a road in four hours. CCC camp director Andrew Tweedie selected a gradual path of about one thousand feet, had his crews clear it of brush and small trees, secured truckloads of cinders from the paper plant in Mechanicville and completed a fine gravel road in time for Roosevelt to sweep up the hill in a big touring car accompanied by his motorcade.[17] The spot, which Roosevelt selected, is where the Visitor Center stands today. "Roosevelt's Road," appropriately, is the paved access to the handicapped parking area.

One of Franklin Roosevelt's early acts as president was to transfer the existing military parks from the War Office to the National Park Service, thus moving that agency from a preserver of landscapes to the keeper of the nation's treasured places.

Even with Roosevelt's keen interest, it took a few years for Saratoga to become a national park, the first in New York State. Finally, with a great deal of lobbying by the Saratoga Historical Society, local Rotarians and much press coverage, the Seventy-fifth Congress passed the bill, PL 576, on May 8, 1938, which Roosevelt was delighted to sign into law on June 1 as the 139th property under the National Park Service's care. But it took until 1941 for New York State to complete all the steps for the formal transfer of 1,429 acres of the Battlefield Park to the federal government.

THE VISITOR CENTER

Although President Roosevelt chose the site in 1940, World War II intervened and funding was tight into the 1950s. The one-and-a-half-story building was constructed in 1962 under the NPS's Mission 66 program. The Visitor Center is situated atop Fraser Hill in the northwestern corner

The Visitor Center, only slightly modified since its construction in 1962, lies unobtrusively on the hilltop. From its east-facing windows and terrace, a sweeping view of the Hudson Valley spreads out for visitors to enjoy. *SNHP.*

of the Saratoga Battlefield site, accessed by a curved path and by gradual steps from the parking lot below. The building offers a sweeping eastern view of a portion of the battlefield, the Hudson River Valley and the hills toward Vermont. It is composed of three interconnected hexagonal sections for offices, displays and presentations, with windows and a terrace to feature the view.

The Visitor Center is a representative example of "Park Service Modern" architecture as adopted for the nearly one hundred visitor centers constructed under Mission 66, using locally available natural construction materials and modern elements in a low, horizontal profile. The combination of those elements produced a building that sits lightly on the landscape, blending with its environment and unobtrusive to the historic battlefield it serves. A small addition, housing a museum and library, was added to the Visitor Center in 1974 as part of its preparation for the bicentennial. The center is located near the entrance to the park and serves as the welcoming station and orientation point for park visitors, as well as the beginning of the park tour road.

The Neilson House was originally built circa 1775 and is a rare, surviving local example of the type of simple one-story vernacular farmhouses that were common during the period before the Revolutionary War. Reconstructed to its original appearance, the house is the iconic image of the Saratoga National Historic Park. *SNHP.*

THE NEILSON HOUSE

The farmhouse of John Neilson is prominently visible at Stop 2 of the Saratoga Battlefield Tour Road and is the only building remaining on the site from the time of the battles of Saratoga. The house's current appearance is the result of two major restoration efforts, the first undertaken by the State of New York in the late 1920s and the second completed by the NPS in 1960. These restorations removed most of the nineteenth- and early twentieth-century alterations and returned the building to its likely original eighteenth-century appearance and location, based on internal physical evidence and information gathered from archaeological excavations of the site.

TOUR ROAD

The locations that tell the story of the battles of October 7 and September 19, 1777 are connected by a paved, one-way tour road constructed between 1958 and 1966. The nine-mile loop road serves as the primary means of experiencing the battlefield and provides visitors the opportunity for a self-guided tour. Beginning at the Saratoga NHP Visitor Center, it contains ten interpretive stops at important sites within the battlefield.

THE SCHUYLER HOUSE

The present Schuyler House at the south end of the village of Schuylerville is the third of that family's dwellings built on this property. The original estate was eighteen thousand acres, one-seventh of the Saratoga Patent, granted in 1684 (but made official in 1708) to Johannes Schuyler. By the time the Revolution reached this region of the Hudson Valley, Philip Schuyler (great-grandson of the original Dutch settler) at forty-four had been relieved as major general in command of the Northern Department of the Continental army, replaced by General Gates. After the British officers dined lavishly in the (second) house, built in 1767, they burned the house and outbuildings down in October 1777 as a military tactic. As soon as they had cleared out, Schuyler had his summer home rebuilt just northeast of the destroyed house in under a month, reusing hardware from the burned building, getting wood from his own sawmill and employing the labor of skilled soldiers under General Gates's command.

Ten years later, General Schuyler had the house renovated and made more elegant as a suitable wedding present for his son, John Bradstreet Schuyler. As John's son was only seven when his father died in 1795, the property was leased until the boy, known as Philip II, was married and ready to assume responsibility for the large farm and associated mills in 1811. This generation of the Schuyler family made a prosperous living on the estate and raised nine children there. Philip II carried out his grandfather's vision by spearheading the effort to construct the Champlain Canal, completed in 1823 to link Lake Champlain to the Hudson River and the Erie Canal. Present-day visitors can take a pleasant walk from the old road in back of the Schuyler House north about a mile and a half along the original canal towpath. The village of Saratoga was renamed Schuylerville in 1831 to honor the family.

Following the economic crisis of 1837, Philip Schuyler suffered financial losses that forced him to subdivide and sell his Saratoga property to settle debts. George Strover, Schuyler's agent, bought the house in 1839. Strover and his descendants occupied the house into the 1940s, maintaining it without adding plumbing, heating or electric lighting.

The history of the Schuyler House is entwined with St. Stephen's Episcopal Church, on the steep hill of Grove Street across the road and Fish Creek. A Strover daughter married physician Charles Payn, who gave the land and helped to finance the building of the church in 1869. Strovers, Paynes and Lowbers (another son-in-law) were active on the church's governing board for decades. Some of the Lowber shares in the Schuyler House were given to the church in the 1940s, when NPS was planning to acquire it. Once again, President Roosevelt kept his eye on Saratoga. He dispatched a memo dated October 12, 1943, to the associate director of the NPS, asking, "What is the latest on the acquisition of the Schuyler house in Schuylerville?" Three weeks later, Secretary of the Interior Harold Ickes responded, detailing difficulties with the family's shares, despite George Lowber's willingness to donate the property. The timing of this correspondence is all the more remarkable when put in the context of war being waged in Europe and in the Pacific, and the president preparing for a conference with Churchill and Stalin.

According to some memos of 1945, adding the Schuyler House to the SNHP was not a unanimously favorable idea; some were still thinking narrowly that the parts of the park should all relate directly to the 1777 battles instead of telling the story of the region.[18] Fortunately, broader thinking prevailed, helped no doubt by Roosevelt's personal interest. Final acquisition of the Schuyler House by the National Park Service had to wait until 1950 when all the permissions for St. Stephen's to divest the property had been cleared by the Episcopal bishop and the Albany Diocese. Then the U.S. Attorney General and Secretary of the Interior Harold Ickes approved purchasing the property for a token $1, determining that the house, assessed at $700, was vacant and suitable only for historical purposes.[19] The present size of the Schuyler Estate

Unit of Saratoga National Historical Park is 62.15 acres, bounded on the north by Fish Creek, on the east by the Hudson River, on the south by privately owned land and on the west by U.S. Highway 4.

The main body of the house is twenty-one by sixty feet, built in the late Georgian/early Federal style, with a square kitchen and a one-story rear addition. The house has brick chimneys on the ridgeline of the north and south ends of the main house roof and on the east end of the kitchen ell. A simple shed roof covers four reproduction brick ovens on the exterior of the kitchen ell's east side.

In addition to the surviving privy, well house and stone well head structures, archaeological explorations have identified the sites of additional outbuildings belonging to this house and to its predecessors, including slave quarters, barns, stables and extensive formal gardens.

After taking possession, the NPS undertook work at the Schuyler House in the mid-1950s to restore it to its likely appearance in 1804, the

The National Park Service has removed many alterations installed by later owners of the Schuyler House, including the two-story piazza shown in this 1936 photograph, in the effort to present the residence as it appeared at the time of General Schuyler's death in 1804. *SSHM.*

year of the general's death. A structural report notes that "painstaking documentary and architectural investigations informed the decisions made in conducting the restoration. The project was an excellent example of the mid-twentieth-century architectural preservation philosophy employed by the NPS at [similar] historically significant properties within the National Park System. Much of the restoration work was based on detailed physical or documentary evidence, such as existing trim, doors, and window sash, early floor plans, and outlines of door and window openings." For example, the wallpaper in the parlor is a replica of paper put on by Philip Schuyler II in preparation for the marriage of his daughter, Ruth, in 1836, shortly before he sold the property. A portion of the original paper is displayed. The total effect conveys a sense of a gentleman's country estate of its period, an experience enhanced during the annual candlelight tours in October under the auspices of costumed guides from the Old Saratoga Historical Association.[20]

VICTORY WOODS

The most recent addition to the Saratoga National Historical Park properties is Victory Woods, a 22.78-acre parcel located in the village of Victory, in the highlands above Fish Creek. The land has been relatively undisturbed for more than two hundred years. Several aboveground remnant military fortification structures discovered during archaeological investigations of the site help historians and visitors better understand the events surrounding Burgoyne's defensive position during the days leading up to his surrender on October 17, 1777. The NPS completed a boardwalk trail and interpretive signage in 2010.

SARATOGA MONUMENT

As recounted in the previous chapter, the State of New York maintained and operated the monument until 1970. The following year, New York representative Carleton J. King, with NPS support, introduced a bill that called for its establishment as a national monument and its inclusion in SNHP. No action was taken on the bill at that time, however, and the

From the top of the Saratoga Monument, one can view Lake George to the north, the Hudson River and Vermont's Green Mountains to the east and the Battlefield Unit and the Catskill Mountains to the south. The eclectic Gothic-style obelisk has undergone numerous repairs and updating and is open to the public in the summer. (Check the website or call the Battlefield for current information.) *SSHM.*

monument was left to deteriorate over the following decade due to nominal maintenance provided by the state. As with the Schuyler House, there were a few voices that objected to adding the "intrusive" nineteenth-century period piece, with "historically inaccurate" bas-relief panels of questionable artistic merit. However, the Schuylerville community had taken the monument to heart, adopting it as the village's symbol, and decision-makers recognized its value as representing the commemorative era.

The goal of including the monument in SNHP was finally realized on July 23, 1980, when the State of New York deeded the monument and its 2.82 acres to the federal government. By that time, the monument's structural condition had created safety concerns that eventually forced its closure in 1987. Congress eventually provided the necessary funding to rehabilitate the monument and its grounds. The large undertaking, which included repointing of the masonry, the construction of a ramp for handicapped access, the replacement of rusted I-beams on some of the viewing platforms and the thorough cleaning of all the statues and plaques, took five years to complete (1997–2001). The NPS reopened the monument to the public in 2002 and constructed a new entrance and parking facility in 2005.

Currently, the Saratoga Battlefield serves primarily as a memorial, educational and recreational space. While many of the fortifications and other man-made features of the battles are no longer extant above ground, many of the important landscape characteristics that played a critical role in determining the location and the outcome of the battles—mostly key terrain and observation points—remain intact and provide a visual understanding of the events and the eventual outcome of the battles. Additionally, the views from important locations remain and further convey the significance of these landscape features.

As of 2012, SNHP is composed of 3,392.42 acres within its authorized boundary, 2,976.00 acres of publicly owned land in four separate locations and 416.00 acres of privately owned land over which the NPS holds scenic or other easements.

Chapter 5

In Their Own Words

BURGOYNE'S DEFENSE TO PARLIAMENT: OPENING OF HIS STATE OF THE EXPEDITION, 1780

The Speech of Lieutenant General Burgoyne, prefatory to his Narrative.

Before I enter upon the narrative, which the precedent of your late proceedings authorizes me to lay before you, I think it a duty to the committee, to promise that I shall trouble them with little other matter than such as may be necessary to elucidate the transactions of the campaign of 1777, in that quarter where I commanded.

I shall keep in mind, that to explain the causes of the disaster at Saratoga is the principal point to which all my evidence ought to lead: but at the same time, I shall take confidence in the justice and benevolence of my hearers, that where arguments in exculpation of the commander can aptly be combined with a faithful representation of facts, they will not be deemed foreign to the main object under their consideration.

Upon these ideas, though some introductory explanations are requisite, I shall suppress the inclination I at first conceived, of stating my conduct from the time, when, conjointly with my honourable friend who took the lead in this enquiry, I was called to the unsolicited and unwelcome service in America: nor will I enumerate the complicated circumstances of private misfortune and ill health under which I pursued it. Prudence, as well as other propriety, is, I confess, consulted in this suppression; for were it seen, that an officer had blended with the respect due to authority, warm, though disinterested personal attachments; that under a persuasion of the honour and integrity of the king's servants, he had united to his zeal for the public cause an interest in their private credit and ambition, would it not be conceived, that his guilt must have been atrocious, beyond all excuse or palliation, to induce the very men to whom his endeavours, and his faculties, such as they were, had been thus devoted, not only completely to desert him, but to preclude him, as far as in them lay, from every means of defence, and if possible, to ruin him in the opinion of the king, the army, and the country?

An earnest desire to save, as much as possible, the time of the committee, would also dissuade me from recurring to any points previous to my instructions which have been discussed upon former occasions; but I find that great stress is till laid to my prejudice upon a paper which found its way to the house during my absence: I mean the private letter to the noble lord, Secretary for the American department, dated 1st January, 1777.

CIRCA 1780 AMERICAN VERSE: "THE FATE OF JOHN BURGOYNE" (ROUGHLY TO THE TUNE OF "YANKEE DOODLE")

By an American author.

When Jack, the king's commander,
Was going to his duty.
Through all the crowd he smiled and bow'd
To every blooming beauty.

The city rung with feats he'd done
In Portugal and Flanders,
And all the town thought he'd be crown'd
The first of Alexanders.

To Hampton Court he first repairs
To kiss great George's hand, sirs;

Then to harangue on state affairs
Before he left the land, sirs.

The Lower House sat mute as mouse
To hear his grand oration;
And all the peers, with loudest cheers,
Proclaimed him to the nation.

Then off he went to Canada,
Next to Ticonderoga,
And quitting those away he goes
Straightway to Saratoga.

With great parade his march he made
To gain his wished for station.
While far and wide his minions hied
To spread his Proclamation.

To such as staid he offers made
Of "pardon on submission;
But savage bands should waste the lands
Of all in opposition."

But ah, the cruel fates of war!
This boasted son of Britain,
When mounting his triumphal car
With sudden fear was smitten.

The sons of Freedom gathered round,
His hostile bands confounded,
And when they'd fain have turned their back
They found themselves surrounded!

In vain they fought, in vain they fled,
Their chief, humane and tender,
To save the rest soon thought it best
His forces to surrender.

Brave St. Clair when he first retired
Knew what the fates portended;
And Arnold and heroic Gates
His conduct have defended.

Thus may America's brave sons
With honor be rewarded,
And the fate of all her foes
The same as here recorded.

Published in Ballads and Poems *(1893), William L. Stone.*

TRAVELOGUE, 1850

From Benson J. Lossing's Pictorial Field Book of the Revolution, *vol. I,* Travels of 1848 *(published 1850).*

INTRODUCTION.

> *Far o'er yon azure main thy view extend,*
> *Where seas and skies in blue confusion blend:*
> *Lo, there a mighty realm, by Heaven design'd.*
> *The last retreat for poor, oppress'd mankind;*
> *Form'd with that pomp which marks the hand divine,*
> *And clothes yon vault, where worlds unnumber'd shine.*
> *Here spacious plains in solemn grandeur spread;*
> *Here cloudy forests cast eternal shade;*
> *Rich valleys wind, the sky-tall mountains brave,*
> *And inland seas for commerce spread the wave*
> *With nobler floods the sea-like rivers roll.*
> *And fairer luster purples round the pole.*
>
> *–Timothy Dwight*

EVERY nation eminent for its refinement, displayed in the cultivation of the arts, had its heroic age; a period when its first physical and moral conquests were achieved, and when rude society, with all its impurities, was fused and refined in the crucible of progress.

When civilization first set up its standard as a permanent ensign in the Western hemisphere, northward of the Bahamas and the great Gulf, and the contests for possession began between the wild Aborigines, who thrust no spade into the soil, no sickle into ripe harvests, and those earnest delvers from the Old World, who came with the light of Christianity to plant a new empire and redeem the wilderness by cultivation, then commenced the heroic age of America. It ended when the work of the Revolution, in the eighteenth century, was accomplished; when the bond of vassalage to Great Britain was severed by her colonies, and when the thirteen confederated States ratified a federal Constitution, and upon it laid the broad foundation of our Republic.

Those ancient civilizations, registered by the stylus of history, were mere gleamings of morning compared with the noontide radiance which now lights up the Western World; and even the more modern nations of Europe, brilliant as they appear, have so many dark spots upon the disk of their enlightenment, that their true glory is really less than that of the waxing Star in the West. These ancient and modern civilizations, now past or at their culminating points, were the results of the slow progress of centuries; the heroic age of America, meteor-like, was brilliant and rapid in its course, occupying the space of only a century and a half of time from the permanent implanting of a British colony, weak and dependent, to the founding of our government, which, like Pallas Athena, was, at its birth, full panoplied, strong, eminently individual in its character, and full of recuperative energies. The head of Britannia was cleft by the Vulcan of the Revolution, and from its teeming brain leaped the full-grown daughter, sturdy and defiant.

I resolved to visit the scenes of the northern campaigns during the summer and early autumn. With the exception of the historic grounds lying around New York and among the Hudson Highlands, the fields of Saratoga, in point of importance and distance, invited the initial visit.

I left New York on the evening of the 24th of July for Poughkeepsie, on the banks of the Hudson, there to be joined by a young lady, my traveling companion for the summer. For many days the hot sun had been unclouded, and neither shower nor dew imparted grateful moisture to town or country.

During the afternoon the barometer indicated a change, and portents of a gathering storm arose in the west. At twilight we entered the great amphitheater of the Highlands, and darkness came down suddenly upon us as a tempest of wind, thunder, and rain burst over the Dunderberg and the neighboring heights. A thunder-storm at night in the Hudson Highlands! It is a scene of grandeur and sublimity vouchsafed to few, and never to be forgotten. The darkness became intense, and echo confused the thunder-peals into one continuous roar. The outlines of the hills disappeared in the gloom, and our vessel seemed the only object wrapped in the bosom of the tempest, except when, at every flash of lightning, high wooded cones, or lofty ranges, or rocky cliffs burst into view like a sudden creation of the Omnipotent fiat, and then melted into chaos again. The storm continued until we passed West Point. The clouds then broke, and as we emerged from the upper gate of the from her pavilion, in beauty and majesty, the winds were quiet, the waters placid, and the starry sky serene, for

"The thunder, tramping deep and loud
Had left no foot-marks there."

The next morning the air was clear and cool as in September. At noon we took passage in one of those floating palaces which are the pride of the Hudson River. What a contrast to the awkward contrivance—the mere germ of the steam-boat of the present day—that gave such glory to Fulton, and astonished the world. Her saloon, like a ducal drawing-room; her table, spread as with a royal banquet; her speed, like that of the swift bird, are all the creations of one generation, and seem like works of magic. Among the passengers there were a few—plain and few indeed—who attracted general attention. They were a remnant of a regiment of Volunteers returning home, weary and spirit-broken, from the battlefields of Mexico. Of the scores who went with them, these alone returned to tell of havoc in battle and slaughter by the deadly *vomito*. They were young, but the lesson of sad experience might be read on each brow, and the natural joy of the homeward-bound beamed not in their eyes. To them military glory was a bubble burst; and the recollections of the recent past brought not to them that joy which the soldier feels who has battled in defense of country and home. At Albany preparations had been made to receive them, and for half a mile the wharves, bridges, vessels, and houses were thickly covered with people anxious to see the returning heroes. We landed with difficulty in the midst of the excitement and noise, for cannon-peals, and drum and fife, and the rattle of military accouterments, and wild huzzas of the crowd, and the coaxing and swearing of porters and coachmen, were enough to confound confusion itself. How changed was the scene when we returned, a few weeks later. Wharves, bridges, and houses had been swept by conflagration, and acres of the dense city were strewn with smoking ruins. [A massive fire struck Albany in August 1848.]

Early on the morning of the 26th we left Albany for Bemis's Heights, near the village of Stillwater. An omnibus ride of an hour, over a fine McAdam road, placed us in Troy, where we took stage for the Waterford ferry at Lansingburgh, four miles above. The day was excessively warm, and eleven passengers occupied "seats for nine." Not a zephyr stirred the waters or the leaves. A funny little waterman, full of wine and wit, or something stronger and coarser, offered to row us across in his rickety skiff. I demanded the price for ferriage.

"Five thousand dollars," hiccoughed the Charon. I did not object to the price, but valuing safety at a higher figure, sought the owner of a pretty craft near by, while the little votary of Bacchus was tugging manfully, but unsuccessfully, at a huge trunk, to lift it into his boat. Before he was fairly conscious that he was not yet toiling at our luggage, we were out upon the stream in the "Lady of the Lake." I compensated the tipsy boatman for his labor of love by a brief temperance lecture; but the seed doubtless fell upon "stony ground," for he had the hard-heartedness to consign me to the safe keeping of him whom

> "The old painters limned with a hoof and a horn,
> A beak and a scorpion tail."

We pushed across the Hudson to the upper mouth or "sprout" of the Mohawk, and, gliding under the rail-road bridge and along a sluice of the Champlain Canal, clambered up a high bank, and reached the packet office at Waterford toward noon. The suppressed roar of Cohoes' Falls, two miles distant, wooed us to the pleasures of that fashionable resort, to while away the three hours before the arrival of the canal packet.

These falls, though not so grand as many others either in volume or altitude of cataract, or in the natural scenery around, nevertheless present many points of beauty and sublimity exceedingly attractive to the tourist. The Mohawk is here more than one hundred yards wide, and perfectly rock-ribbed on both sides. The fall is nearly seventy feet perpendicular, in addition to the turbulent rapids above and below. A bridge, eight hundred feet long, spans the river half a mile below the falls, from which a fine view may be obtained of the whole scene.

Before entering the Hudson, the river is divided into four mouths or sprouts, as they are called, by three rocky islands. Haver's, Van Schaick's or Cohoes', and Green's or Tibbetts's Islands, which form a scene that is singularly picturesque. It is generally supposed that Henry Hudson, the discoverer of the river bearing his name, ascended as far as this point in 1609, and that he and his boat's crew were the first white men who beheld the cataract of Cohoes.

Among the dramatic stories circulated was that of Jane McCrea, a cause célèbre for the Revolution. It was reported that when she went in search of her Tory beau, she was scalped and killed by Burgoyne's rogue Indians under this fabled tree in Fort Edward *Lossing.*

The ruins of Fort Ticonderoga always were an attraction, perhaps in 1850 evoking Gothic visions popular at the time. *SNHP.*

The mouth of the Mohawk was a point of much interest toward the close of the summer of 1777, when Van Schaick's Island was fortified by General Schuyler, then in command of the northern division of the Continental army. Properly to understand the position of affairs at that period, it is necessary to take a brief view of events immediately antecedent to, and intimately connected with, the military operations at this point, and at Stillwater a few weeks later.

Incensed at the audacity of the American Congress in declaring the colonies free and independent states; piqued at the consummate statesmanship displayed by the members of that Congress, and foiled in every attempt to cajole the Americans by delusive promises, or to crush the spirit of resistance by force of arms, the British ministry, backed by the stubborn king and a strong majority in both Houses of Parliament, determined to open the campaign of 1777 with such vigor, and to give to the service in America such material, as should not fail to put down the rebellion by midsummer, and thus vindicate British valor, which seemed to be losing its invincibility.

1877 SARATOGA MONUMENT DEDICATION

On the occasion of the laying of the cornerstone of the Saratoga Monument.

All was decided here, and at this hour
Our sun leaped up, though clouds still veiled its power.
From Saratoga's hills we date the birth—
Our Nation's birth among the powers of earth.
Not back to '76, New Yorkers' date—
The mighty impulse launched our "Ship of State"
'Twas given here—where shines our rising sun
Excelsior! These hills saw victory won.
This vale the cradle where the colonies
Grew into States—despite all enemies.
Yes, on this spot—Thanks to our gracious God
Where last in conscious arrogance it trod,
Defil'd as captives Burgoyne's conquered horde;
Below their general yielded up his sword.
There to our flag bowed England's, battle-torn.
Where now we stand th' United States was born.

J. Watts De Peyster
October 17, 1877

1919: LOCAL HISTORY OF A SIEGE

The "Story of Old Saratoga" carries over the style that predominated much of nineteenth-century American writing. John Brandow was the minister at the Dutch Reformed Church in Schuylerville.

Third Period of the Campaign—The Retreat

Burgoyne now finding his position on the heights untenable, withdrew his army during the night of the 7th to the low ground near the river, retaining, however, so much of the high ground as lies immediately north of the Wilbur's Basin ravine. His leading generals urged him to abandon his heavy artillery and unnecessary camp equipage and push with all speed for Canada. But No! life on the way would not have been worth the living without that precious park of artillery, his generous stock of liquors, and his packs of showy millinery; so all must be risked that they might be kept.[21]

If Burgoyne could have brought himself to abandon everything except necessities, as did St. Clair when he evacuated Ticonderoga, or as did Morgan and his men in 1775 who, in their light equipment, made 600 miles in twenty-one days from Winchester, Va., to Boston, he could have crossed to the east side of the Hudson on his floating bridge, and, made Ticonderoga without a question, and saved his army; for Gates at that time had not a sufficient force at the north to materially obstruct him.

The ancients had a saying, "Whom the gods propose to destroy they first make mad." While a commission of lunacy would hardly have voted General Burgoyne *non compos mentis*, yet for the next few days his behavior was so lacking in sound sense and vigorous action that had he been really mad he could not have compassed the ruin of his army with greater certainty or celerity than he did.

General Fraser died the next morning after the battle. Before his death he requested that he might be buried at 6 p.m. within the Great Redoubt on the second hill north of Wilbur's Basin. This hill had been with him a favorite spot on account of the beauty of the view. Such a request proves that General Fraser was not himself, or that he did not realize the situation when he made it. It was no time for Burgoyne to take counsel of sentiment, yet he resolved to fulfill the dying soldier's request to the letter; so he spent that, to him, precious day in preparing leisurely for retreat and in sharp skirmishes with the advanced lines of the Americans who had occupied his old camp ground.

On this day General Lincoln, who had command of the American right, while personally leading a body of militia to take post near the enemy on the river flats, fell in with an advanced party of Germans in a thick wood. Mistaking them for Americans, because of their blue uniforms, he approached within a short distance of them before he discovered his error. At once he wheeled his horse and, as he did so, they fired a volley, and a shot fractured his leg. He escaped and was carried back to his quarters.[22]

Wilkinson writes that the same day (the 8th): "The enemy refused a flag with which I attempted, at every point of his line, to convey a letter to Lady Harriet Ackland from her husband, a prisoner in our hands."

Death of Fraser. General Fraser was evidently the idol of the army, for among other eulogists, Lieut. Anbury in his Travels, has this to say of him: "Gen. Fraser was brought back to camp on his horse, a grenadier on each side supporting him. The officers all anxious and eagerly inquiring as to his wound—the downcast look and melancholy that was visible to every one as to his situation, and all the answer he could make to the many inquiries was a shaking of the head, expressive that it was all over with him. So much was he beloved that not only officers and soldiers, but all the women, flocked around solicitous for his fate."

General Fraser died in a small farm house which at the time was occupied by the Baroness Riedesel, wife of the General of the German contingent. The house was located near the foot of the hill whereon he was buried. When the road was changed it was moved and stood on the present highway near the river till 1873, when it was torn down. The Baroness in her Memoirs gives a touching account of the death of the General.

On the morning of the 7th, before the reconnaissance and battle, Generals Burgoyne, Phillips, and Fraser had promised to dine with herself and husband, and she was still waiting for them when General Fraser was brought in on a litter mortally wounded. Afterward, when told that his hurt was fatal and that he had but a few hours to live, she heard him exclaim repeatedly and sadly: "Oh fatal ambition! Poor General Burgoyne! My poor wife!" Then he frequently begged the Baroness' pardon for causing her so much trouble, because he was laid in her apartment, and she was so assiduous in her efforts to add to his comfort. His brave spirit took its departure at eight o'clock a.m. of the 8th. The corpse having been washed and wrapped in a sheet, was laid on the bed and she, with her three children, was obliged to remain in the room most of the day.

Precisely at 6 p.m. he was carried by his beloved grenadiers to the spot he had selected for his sepulcher, accompanied by the chaplain Brudenell, the generals and all other officers whose duties would permit them to be present. The Americans noticing the procession, and imagining that some hostile movement was on foot, opened a battery upon them. The balls flew thick and fast, some of them tearing up the ground and scattering the dirt over the participants during the ceremony; but fortunately their aim was high and all the shots went wild.

Burgoyne Describes Fraser's Burial. Burgoyne's eloquent description of the burial of Fraser is well worthy of a place here. He says: "The incessant cannonading during the solemnity, the steady attitude and unaltered voice with which the chaplain officiated, though frequently covered with dust, which the shot threw up on all sides of him, the mute but expressive mixture of sensibility and indignation upon the mind of every man who was present, the growing duskiness added to the scenery, and the whole marked a juncture of such character that would make one of the finest subjects for the pencil of a master that the field ever exhibited. To the canvas and to the pen of a more important historian, gallant friend, I consign thy memory. There may thy talents, thy manly virtues, their progress and their period find due distinction, and long may they survive, after the frail record of my pen shall be forgotten."

Retreat and Delay at Coveville. After the burial service was fittingly closed, Burgoyne issued orders for the retreat, an order sadly at variance with his grandiloquent announcement of three months agone that "this army must not retreat." He felt obliged to leave behind him his hospital, with some four hundred sick and wounded, whom he commended to the tender mercies of General Gates and his insurrectionists. His confidence in their humanity was not misplaced, for as soon as he learned of it Gates sent forward a body of light horse to protect the sick and wounded from insult and plunder.

It was nine o'clock before the army got under way. During the night a pouring rain set in, which, together with the inky darkness and the narrow road, and the in-ability of the poor horses, weakened by starvation, to pull the loads, permitted only a snail's pace movement. Burgoyne reached Dovegat [Coveville] about 4 a.m., the same hour that his rear guard left Wilbur's Basin, or two hours before day, when he ordered a halt. It was generally supposed that this was for the better concentration of the army, and that they would move on again shortly; but, to the unspeakable chagrin and disgust of the whole army, the delay was protracted till 4 p.m. before the retreat was resumed. This was a criminal blunder under the circumstances, for not only was much precious time lost but the continued rain rendered the roads so soft that further movement with his artillery and baggage train was well nigh impossible. As a result he was obliged to abandon most of his tents and camp equipage, which, by the way proved a most acceptable contribution to the comfort of the Americans, who promptly appropriated such as were not too badly damaged by the fire set by Burgoyne's orders.

During this interval of twelve hours the British army was strung along from within a mile of Saratoga to below Coveville, General Riedesel in charge of the advance and General Phillips bringing up the rear.

Digby in his Journal says: "During our march [retreat] it surprised us their not placing troops on the heights we were obliged to pass under, [i.e. the bluffs which for a long way overlook the river flats] as by so doing we must have suffered much." Others likewise have wondered much about the same thing. On the 8th a Brigade marched through the woods nearly to Saratoga, and returned. Why were there not other Brigades sent forward to harass the enemy on the 9th? We have not been able to discover any sufficient reason, except rain, and Gates' lack of initiative, for such failure to improve an opportunity.

Woes of the Bateaumen. Burgoyne's bateaumen on their retreat up river were greatly annoyed by the American militiamen, who posted themselves along the bank to waylay them. An interesting writer who, as a boy, native to this locality, followed up Gates' army after the battles "to see what was going on," relates the following incident in this connection: "A few bateaux and scows were passing along as I arrived—they were loaded with military stores, the baggage of the officers, and the women who followed their 'soger laddies.' A few well directed shots brought them to the bank. A rush took place for the prey. Everything was hauled out and carried back into a low swampy place in the rear, and a guard placed over it. When the plunder was divided among the captors, the poor females, trembling with fear, were released and permitted to go oft' in a boat to the British army, a short distance above. Such a collection of tanned and leathern visages was never before seen. Poorly clad, their garments ragged, and their persons war-worn and weary, those women were objects of my sincere pity."[23]

Lady Ackland's Adventure. While Burgoyne was delaying at Dovegat, there occurred one of those incidents which display in the most engaging light the heroic fortitude of womankind under the most trying conditions, particularly in cases where her affections are involved.

The heroine on this occasion was the Lady Harriet Ackland, before mentioned, wife of Major John Dyke Ackland, of the grenadiers. She had already nursed him back to health in a miserable hut at Chambly, in Canada, and afterward when she heard that he was wounded at the battle of Hubbardton, Vt., she, contrary to his injunctions, came up the lake to Skenesborough (Whitehall) with the determination not to leave him again. From there she shared his tent through all the vicissitudes of the campaign. Judge then of her state of mind when word was brought from the field that her husband was mortally wounded and a prisoner in the hands of the Americans. After spending two nights and a day in an agony of suspense, she resolved to ask General Burgoyne for permission to go over to the enemy's camp to seek out and care for her husband. She was urged to this step also by the Baroness Riedesel. Burgoyne was astounded by such a request from a woman of her quality at such a time, and especially as she was then in a most delicate condition. Finally he yielded to her importunities, furnished her with a boat and crew, and allowed the chaplain Brudenell—he of the steady nerves—and her husband's valet who still carried a ball in his shoulder received in the late action, to accompany her, and then armed with a letter of commendation from Burgoyne to Gates, she set out in the edge of evening, during a storm of wind and rain, on her venturesome trip. She reached the American advanced pickets about ten o'clock, and being hailed, went ashore, where she was courteously received and hospitably lodged for the night by Major Dearborn, who was able to relieve her mind with the assurance that her husband was in a most comfortable and hopeful condition. In the morning she passed on down the river to Bemis Heights, where she was met and most graciously received by General Gates, whence she was taken to her husband, who was lodged in the roomy tent of one Joseph Bird. General Burgoyne's letter to Gates in her behalf, though written in haste and on a piece of dirty wet paper, has ever been regarded as a model of gracefulness and point in epistolary literature. Here it is:

"Sir:

Lady Harriet Ackland, a Lady of the first distinction by family, rank, and by personal virtues, is under such concern on account of Major Ackland, her husband,

wounded and a prisoner in your hands, that I cannot
refuse her request to commit her to your protection.

Whatever general impropriety there may be in persons acting in your situation and mine to solicit favors,
I cannot see the uncommon perseverance in every female
grace, and exaltation of character of this Lady, and her
very hard fortune, without testifying that your attentions
to her will lay me under obligation.

I am. Sir,

Your obedient servant,

October 9, 1777. J. Burgoyne.

Major General Gates."[24]

Fellows Anticipates Burgoyne's Retreat to Saratoga. General
Gates, in anticipation of an early retreat on the part of Burgoyne had
sent forward General Fellows, before the battle of the 7th, with thirteen
hundred men to occupy the heights of Saratoga, north of Fish creek
(whereon Schuylerville stands) to waylay stragglers and dispute the
passage of the creek with any advanced parties of the enemy that might
be sent forward. The day after the battle the Americans discovering signs
that the British were preparing to decamp, Gates sent two messengers,
one on each side of the river, to apprise Fellows of the probable movement
and order him to recross the Hudson and defend the ford. This ford was
located at the upper end of the island over which the Schuylerville and
Greenwich highway bridge now passes. Before this notice reached him
General Fellows had a narrow escape from surprise and possible capture.

On the night of the 8th, and some hours before his army started,
Burgoyne had sent forward Lieutenant Colonel Sutherland with a scout
to make observations. He discovered Fellows' situation, and guided by the
fires, he completely encircled his camp without once being challenged.
He hastened back and begged Burgoyne to allow him to go on with his
regiment and attack him, assuring him that since they lay there unguarded

he could capture the whole body. Burgoyne refused peremptorily; but had he permitted it, in all probability, Sutherland would have succeeded. The reasons for the refusal were probably, first, because he had no men to lose, and secondly, he had neither place nor provender for so large a body had they been captured.

At four o'clock p.m. on the 9th, the British army was again set in motion, and wading the now swollen Fish creek, bivouacked wet, shivering and hungry, without tents or covering, on the cold wet ground. They were over just in time to see the rear of General Fellows' detachment ascend the eastern bank of the Hudson and place himself in a position to bar their passage that way and to take possession of their old camp north of the Battenkill. Previously to his withdrawal across the Hudson, Fellows destroyed the bridge over Fish creek.[25]

Burgoyne did not forget to make himself very comfortable that night, though his men were most miserable. He remained on the south side of the creek and occupied the Schuyler mansion, retaining Hamilton's brigade as a body guard. The officers with their men slept on the cold, wet ground, with nothing to protect them but oil-cloth. Nor did the wives of the officers fare any better.

Discomforts of the Ladies. Supposing that Burgoyne's advance to Albany would be little else than a triumphal march, with but feeble opposition to overcome, these fine ladies, with adventurous spirit, had come along to enjoy a novel excursion and picnic, and, incidentally, to select for themselves a fine mansion from the estates sure to be confiscated from the rebels. Among these were Lady Ackland, as we have seen, and the Baroness Riedesel, wife of the General (pronounced Re-day-zel; the British soldiers called him Red-hazel), a woman of rare culture, intellectual force, and vivacity of spirit, and withal possessed of unusual literary ability. Colonel Wilkinson, Gates' adjutant general, speaks of her as "the amiable, the accomplished and dignified baroness." She was accompanied by her children, three little girls. The oldest was Augusta, 4 years and 7 months; the 2d Frederika, 2 years; and 3d Caroline, 10 weeks old when they started.[26]

Of her experiences on this particular night she writes: "Toward evening, we at last came to Saratoga, which was only half an hour's march from the place where we had spent the whole day. I was wet through and through by the frequent rains, and was obliged to remain in this condition the entire night, as I had no place whatever where I could change my linen. I, therefore, seated myself before a good fire, and undressed my children; after which, we laid ourselves down together upon some straw. I asked General Phillips, who came up to where we were, why we did not continue our retreat while there was yet time, as my husband had pledged himself to cover it, and bring the army through? 'Poor woman,' answered he, 'I am amazed at you! Completely wet through, have you still the courage to wish to go further in this weather? Would that you were only our commanding general! He halts because he is tired, and intends to spend the night here, and give us a supper.' In this latter achievement, especially, General Burgoyne was very fond of indulging. He spent half the nights in singing and drinking, and amusing himself with the wife of a commissary, who was his mistress, and who as well as he loved champagne."

The Marshall House Cannonaded. Early in the morning of October 8th, General Gates, expecting that Burgoyne would retreat, had ordered General Bailey, with 900 New Hampshire troops, to cross the Hudson and hasten to the aid of General Fellows, opposite Saratoga. Captain Furnival was ordered to follow with his battery. The same evening they were reinforced by a Massachusetts regiment under Colonel Mosley. On the evening of the 9th Captain Furnival was ordered to cross the Battenkill and erect some earthworks. This battery was placed on the hills north of Clark's Mills, and was erected during the night of the 9th of October.[27]

General Matoon, then a lieutenant of this company, relates that on the morning of the 10th, "seeing a number of officers on the steps of a house [the Marshall House] opposite, on a hill a little north of the mouth of the Battenkill surveying our works, we opened fire on them. I leveled our guns and with such effect as to disperse them. We took the house to be their headquarters. We continued our fire till a nine or twelve pounder was brought to bear on us, and rendered our works untenable."

This battery, in company with a Massachusetts regiment, was then ordered to Fort Edward to defend the fording place there, which they did effectually till recalled on the 14th, after the armistice was declared.[28]

There was no more cannonading from this hill during the siege of Burgoyne.

On the 10th the force of General Fellows on the east side of the Hudson was augmented to three thousand, made up of New Hampshire and Massachusetts troops, chiefly militia.

The Siege. Burgoyne waded Fish Creek the morning of the 10th, dragged across his heavy artillery, and seeing that it was now too late to cross the river at the Battenkill, took up the positions he had determined upon on the 14th of September, in case of an attack at that time. He erected a fortified camp on Prospect Hill, or the heights of Saratoga, as it was then called. This camp began north of the house of Counsellor William S. Ostrander, and embraced Prospect Hill Cemetery, also the land between the cemetery and the terrace—east of George M. Watson's orchard and extended south into the Victory woods. Part of the 20th, and six companies of the 47th regiment, with the German grenadiers and Berner's battalion, had their camp on the flat where Green and Pearl streets now run and north of Burgoyne street. The German Yagers (riflemen) and Canadians camped each side of the Saratoga road on the flat or terrace above the Boston & Maine R.R. station. The balance of the 20th British regiment, and the Germans under Riedesel, occupied the ground north of Spring street, bounded on the east by Broadway and on the west by a line running north from Dr. Webster's house and reaching toward the Marshall house. The artillery was parked on the spur of high ground east of Broadway and on the continuation of Spring Street, now called Seeleyville.

The same day (the 10th) Burgoyne sent forward a working party made up chiefly of loyalists, under Capt. Mackey, to repair roads and bridges, also a detachment of the 47th Regt., all under Lieut. Col. Sutherland. They were also to learn if the enemy had occupied Ft. Edward and, if feasible, to build a bridge and take possession of the fort. Sutherland sent back word that he had met none of the enemy, and that the bridge was already building. His express had not reached Saratoga before the Colonel received orders to return to camp with his force. He at once started with the regulars, but left Mackey with his company to continue work on the bridge. Soon a large party of Americans appeared on the Ft. Edward side and put an end to their bridge building. About then Capt. Mackey and his Provincials, and the few Indians with him, discovered that Canada was a far more attractive place than Saratoga, so they struck for the north. Sutherland was recalled because Burgoyne had been apprised of an attack by the Americans.

Gates Tardy Pursuit. Through some mismanagement in the commissary department, Gates could not immediately follow up the advantage which the victory of the 7th gave him. In consequence of this, his main body was not ready for the pursuit till about noon of the 10th. The road and fields on the way northward were found to be strewed with abandoned wagons and carts, carcasses of horses starved or driven to death, ammunition, tents and every sort of baggage, all of which had been purposely damaged. Besides this the bridges had been destroyed, and many of the buildings along the way had been burned. Among these were the fine dwelling and all outbuildings of Col. Cornelius Van Veghten at Coveville.

Colonel Wilkinson in his "Memoirs" says: "It rained and the army did not march until the afternoon; our front reached Saratoga about four o'clock, where we discovered the British army encamped on the heights beyond the Fish creek, General Fellows' corps on the opposite bank of the river, and the bateaux of the enemy at the mouth of the creek, with a fatigue party busily employed unloading and conveying their contents across the plain to the heights. The commanding officer of artillery, Major Stevens, ready to improve every advantage, ran a couple of light pieces down on the plain near the river, and opened a battery upon the bateaux and working party at the landing, which soon dispersed it; but he drew the fire of the enemy's whole park upon him from the heights, which obliged him to retire after the loss of a tumbrel [ammunition cart], which was blown up by a shot from the enemy, and caused a shout from the whole British army."

"The army took a position in the wood on the heights in several lines, their right resting on the brow of the hill, about a mile in the rear of the Fish creek, Colonel Morgan being in front and near the church."[29]

The same authority says that Gates appropriated a small hovel about ten feet square with a dirt floor for his headquarters. It was located at the foot of a hill, along the road something over a mile south of Fish Creek.

After Gates had posted his army south of the creek, Burgoyne ordered the Schuyler mansion, with the mills and other outbuildings, to be set on fire. These with their contents were valued at $50,000.

Gates' Abortive Attack. That same evening (the 10th) word came to Gates that Burgoyne had gone on toward Fort Edward, and that only a guard was left behind with the baggage. His informant had mistaken the two regiments sent ahead for the whole army. Gates at once issued orders for the entire force to cross the creek in the morning and assault the British camp under cover of the fog, which usually rises from the river and remains till after sunrise at that season of the year.

Burgoyne in some way received notice of this proposed assault and posted his men to the best advantage to receive it.

Agreeably to orders, Morgan crossed the creek at Victory Mills, below the old dam at the stone bridge, and advancing through the fog soon fell in with a British picket, which fired and cut down a lieutenant and two privates. This led him to think that there must be some mistake about the retreat of the British, which misgiving he reported to Colonel Wilkinson, who came up at this moment. As a result Generals Learned and Patterson were sent to his support with their brigades.

Wilkinson then hastening down to the right, learned from a deserter, and from a squad of thirty-five of the enemy just captured, that Burgoyne had not retreated, but was posted and awaiting the American attack. At once he dispatched an aide to Gates with the message: "Tell the General, that his own fame and the interests of the cause are at hazard; that his presence is necessary with the troops." But in obedience to orders, Nixon's and part of [Brigadier General John] Glover's brigades had forded the creek and were deploying for action; Captain Nathan Goodale, of Putnam's regiment, swung to the right and captured a party of sixty men at the mouth of the creek and also the bateaux they were guarding.[30]

Suddenly the fog lifted and disclosed to their astonished gaze the whole British army drawn up and ready to give them a fiery greeting. They at once opened with musketry and cannon upon the Americans who, realizing their ugly situation at a glance, broke for the south side of the creek, without much regard as to the order of their going.

Wilkinson fearing that the left might be badly entrapped, hastened up and found Morgan and Learned within two hundred yards of Burgoyne's strongest position on Prospect Hill, and just entering ground which had been cleared by the enemy in front of their works. He found Learned near the center and begged him to halt, which he did. Wilkinson said to him (quoting from his Memoirs), "'You must retreat,' Learned asked me, 'have you orders?' I answered, 'I have not, as the exigency of the case did not allow me time to see General Gates.' He observed, 'Our brethren are engaged on the right, and the standing order is to attack.' I informed him 'our troops on the right have retired, and the fire you hear is from the enemy'; and, I added, 'although I have no orders for your retreat, I pledge my life for the General's approbation.'" Several field officers coming up and approving the proposition, the order for the retreat was given. They were hardly turned when the British, who had been quietly awaiting the assault, fired a volley and killed several men, among whom was an officer.

Thus Gates got out of a tight place, and escaped dire disaster, by a very narrow margin. Had he been the great general that his friends pictured him, he would not have ordered such an attack without knowing for a certainty whether the main body of his enemy had decamped or not. He would also have been near the front, when the attack began that he might be able quickly to recall or give new orders as the exigency might demand. For this escape, as for his victories, Gates could thank his subordinates. He never allowed his sacred person to be seen along danger lines if he could avoid it. Only once during the Revolution was he under fire, at Camden, S.C., and then he beat the record in getting away, for he made two hundred miles on horseback in three days.

Burgoyne had hoped great things from this move on the part of Gates, feeling sure that he could annihilate the assaulting force, but was sorely disappointed at the outcome. He described it as "one of the most adverse strokes of fortune during the campaign."

Gates Decides Upon a Regulation Siege. Gates now decided to starve Burgoyne into a surrender by siege, rather than compel him by force of arms as some of his officers urged, thus avoiding much bloodshed. He at once took steps to make sure of his prey by completing his lines of circumvallation. Morgan and his Virginians, Learned's brigade, and a Pennsylvania force occupied the high ground to the west of Burgoyne. Their lines stretched from the creek, up back of the Victory school house, through the French burying ground, in the rear of the house now owned and occupied by Mr. David H. Craw, and along the elevated ridge to the north. The east side of the river was held by New Hampshire, Massachusetts and Connecticut troops, while New York, New England

and New Jersey held the south. New Hampshire and Vermont, under the redoubtable Stark, a day or two later filled the gap to the north, and so practically corked the bottle. Thus New England, the Middle and Southern States were all represented at that crucial moment in our national history, and all very appropriately had a share in the decisive stroke that determined the severance of these colonies from the mother country, and assured their independence.

But as late as the 12th there was still a chance for Burgoyne to escape. There was an opening northward on the west side of the river, as it had not yet been occupied by our people. He called a council of his generals, laid the situation before them, and asked their advice. Riedesel strongly urged that they should leave artillery and baggage behind, and, thus lightened, attempt to escape by avoiding Fort Edward, now held by the Americans, cross four miles above, and strike for Ticonderoga through the woods on the west of Lake George. Orders were at once issued to move out that night if the provisions could be distributed by ten or eleven o'clock. Precisely at ten o'clock Riedesel notified Burgoyne that the provisions had been distributed, and everything was ready, when he and all the rest were astonished to receive orders to stay where they were, as it was now too late. What decided him that it was "too late" is not known. But when the morning broke, sure enough, it was too late; for during the night Stark and his men had crossed the river just above the mouth of the Battenkill on rafts, occupied the gap and erected a battery on a hill (probably the bare one back of Mr. D.A. Bullard's farm buildings). This was the springing of "the trap," about which General Riedesel had talked, the corking of the bottle which sealed the fate of the British army.

They were now completely surrounded. Gates had thrown a floating bridge across the Hudson below Fish creek. The approach to this bridge was just below the mouth of the deep ditch that runs east from Chubb's bridge. This gave easy communication with Fellows to the east; and on this with the raft just built above. Gates could pass in safety all around his foe, if he dared.

The Americans now made it very warm for the Britons. Fellows' batteries on the bluffs, east of the river, were echoed by Gates' from the heights south of Victory, and then the new battery on the hill to the north bellowed Amen! we are with you! while Morgan's sharpshooters to the west, and the Yankee marksmen everywhere else popped at any hostile head that dared show itself from behind a tree, or above the breastworks. All this, with the answering thunder of Burgoyne's heavy artillery, must have made terrific music, such as these Saratoga hills never heard before nor since.

Woes of the Besieged. The experiences of those shut within this fiery and thunderous arena whereon Schuylerville now stands, must have been appalling beyond description. There were but few places of safety except behind trees, in a few hollows, or immediately behind breastworks. Hundreds of dead horses and oxen lay everywhere, which had been killed by cannon or musket shots, or which had died from starvation. Without hospital tents or any hospital conveniences, the sick and wounded soldiers would drag themselves to some sheltered spot and there breathe out their lives in agony on the cold, damp ground. There were but few places where the surgeons could dress the wounds without being interrupted by cannon shot dropping or crashing through the trees. Fellows' battery on the bluffs opposite Schuylerville was especially annoying to the British, and they were unable to silence it. It was from thence that the Marshall house was chiefly cannonaded;[31] from there the shot was fired that carried off the ham from Burgoyne's table, and so broke up one of his dinner parties,[32] and thence the cannon ball came that lodged in an oak tree by the side of which General Burgoyne was standing.[33] No soldier dare lay aside his arms even to sleep. There was constant firing on the picket lines, and a man on duty there hardly dared show himself from behind a tree, or his head above a rifle pit, lest a whistling bullet should perforate him. And though there were rivers of water all about, yet for those beleaguered Britons there was hardly a drop to drink.

A few springs and the rivulets running down the hills could not supply the needs of six thousand men with their horses and cattle. Any man who attempted to reach the creek or river became a mark for a dozen rifles. Some of the wives of the common soldiers risked a trip to the river with their buckets for water, and found the Americans too chivalrous to harm a woman. And, by the way, there were no braver hearts in that army than beat in the breasts of those women. Baroness de Riedesel tells of one who supplied the occupants of the Marshall house, and how they rewarded her.

Baroness Riedesel Relates Her Experiences. The account given by that most estimable lady of her experiences in the Marshall house are of so interesting and thrilling a character that we should wrong our readers not to allow her to tell them her own story. She proved herself to be a veritable angel of mercy to those poor officers and men, yes a forerunner of Florence Nightingale, Clara Barton and the Red Cross. She writes:

"About two o'clock in the afternoon [of the tenth], the firing of cannon and small arms was again heard, and all was alarm and confusion. My husband sent me a message telling me to betake myself forthwith into a house not far from there. I seated myself in the calash with my children, and had scarcely driven up to the house when I saw on the opposite side of the Hudson river five or six men with guns, which were aimed at us. Almost involuntarily I threw the children on the bottom of the calash and myself over them. At the same instant the churls fired, and shattered the arm of a poor English soldier behind us, who was already wounded and was also retreating into the house. Immediately after our arrival a frightful cannonade began, principally directed against the house in which we had sought shelter, probably because the enemy believed, from seeing so many people flocking around it, that all the generals made it their headquarters.[34] Alas! it harbored none but wounded soldiers, or

Baroness von Riedesel and her children escaped injury by seeking shelter in the basement of the Marshall House during an American artillery attack. *Lossing.*

women! We were finally obliged to take refuge in a cellar, in which I laid myself down in a corner not far from the door. My children lay down on the earth with their heads upon my lap, and in this manner we passed the entire night. A horrible stench, the cries of the children, and yet more than all this, my own anguish, prevented me from closing my eyes. On the following morning [the eleventh], the cannonade again began, but on a different side.[35] I advised all to go out of the cellar for a little while, during which time I would have it cleaned, as otherwise we would all be sick.

They followed my suggestion, and I at once set many hands to work, which was in the highest degree necessary; for the women and children being afraid to venture forth, had soiled the whole cellar. After they had all gone out and left me alone, I for the first time surveyed our place of refuge. It consisted of three beautiful cellars, splendidly arched. I proposed that the most dangerously wounded of the officers should be brought into one of them; that the women should remain in another; and that all the rest should stay in the third, which was nearest the entrance. I had just given the cellars a good sweeping, and had fumigated them by sprinkling vinegar on burning coals, and each one had found his place prepared for him—when a fresh and terrible cannonade threw us all once more into alarm. Many persons, who had no right to come in, threw themselves against the door. My children were already under the cellar steps, and we would all have been crushed, if God had not given me strength to place myself before the door, and with extended arms prevent all from coming in; otherwise every one of us would have been severely injured. Eleven cannon balls went through the house, and we could plainly hear them rolling over our heads. One poor soldier (a British surgeon by the name of Jones), whose leg they were about to amputate, having been laid upon a table for this purpose, had the other leg taken off by another cannon ball, in the midst of the operation. His comrades all ran off, and when they again came back they found him in one corner of the room, where he had rolled in his anguish, scarcely breathing. I was more dead than alive, though not so much on account of our own danger, as for that which enveloped my husband, who, however, frequently sent to see how I was getting along, and to tell me that he was still safe.

The wife of Major Harnage, a Madam Reynels, the wife of the good lieutenant who the day previous had so kindly shared his broth with me, the wife of a commissary, and myself, were the only ladies who were with the army.[36] We sat together bewailing our fate, when one came in, upon which they all began whispering, looking at the same time exceedingly sad. I noticed this, and also that they cast silent glances toward me. This awakened in my mind the dreadful thought that my husband had been killed. I shrieked aloud, but they assured me that this was not so, at the same time intimating to me by signs, that it was the lieutenant—the husband of our companion—who had met with misfortune. A moment after she was called out. Her husband was not yet dead, but a cannon ball had taken off his arm close to the shoulder. During the whole night we heard his moans, which resounded fearfully through the vaulted cellars. The poor man died toward morning. We spent the remainder of this night as the former ones. In the meantime my husband came to visit me, which lightened my anxiety and gave me fresh courage. On the following morning [the twelfth], however, we got things better regulated. Major Harnage, his wife, and Mrs. Reynels made a little room in a corner, by hanging curtains from the ceiling. They wished to fix up for me another corner in the same manner, but I preferred to remain near the door, so that in case of fire I could rush out from the room. I had some straw brought in and laid my bed upon it, where I slept with my children—my maids sleeping not far from us. Directly opposite us three English officers were quartered—wounded it is true, but, nevertheless resolved not to be left behind in case of a retreat. One of these was Captain Green, aide-de-camp of General Phillips, a very valuable and agreeable man. All three assured me, upon their oaths, that in case of a hasty retreat, they would not leave me, but would each take one of my children upon his horse. For myself one of my husband's horses constantly stood saddled and in readiness. Often my husband wished to withdraw me from danger, by sending me to the Americans; but I remonstrated with him on the ground that to be with people whom I would be obliged to treat with courtesy, while perhaps, my husband was being killed by them, would be even yet more painful than all I was now suffering. He promised me, therefore, that I should henceforward follow the army. Nevertheless, I was often in the night filled with anxiety lest he should march away. At such times I have crept out of my cellar to reassure myself, and if I saw the troops lying around the fires (for the nights were already cold), I would return and sleep quietly. On the third day, I found an opportunity for the first time to change my linen, as my companions had the courtesy to give up to me a little corner; the three wounded officers meanwhile standing guard not far off. Our cook saw to our meals, but we were in want of water; and in order to quench our thirst, I was often obliged to drink wine, and give it also to the children. The continued danger in which my husband was encompassed, was a constant source of anxiety to me. I was the only one of all the women whose husband had not been killed or wounded, and I often said to myself—"shall I be the only fortunate one?"

As the great scarcity of water continued, we at last found a soldier's wife who had the courage to bring water from the river, for no one else would undertake it, as the enemy shot at every man who approached the river. This woman, however, they never molested; and they told us afterward that they spared her on account of her sex.

I endeavored to divert my mind from my troubles, by constantly busying myself with the wounded. I made them tea and coffee, and received in return a thousand benedictions. Often, also, I shared my noon day meal with them. One day a Canadian officer came into our cellar who could scarcely stand up. We at last got it out of him that he was almost dead with hunger. I considered myself very fortunate to have it in my power to offer him my mess. This gave him renewed strength, and gained for me his friendship. One of our greatest annoyances was the stench of the wounds when they began to suppurate.

One day I undertook the care of Major Bloomfield, adjutant to General Phillips, through both of whose cheeks a small musket ball had passed, shattering his teeth and grazing his tongue. He could hold nothing whatever in his mouth. The matter from the wound almost choked him, and he was unable to take any other nourishment except a little broth, or something liquid. We had Rhine wine. I gave him a bottle of it, in hopes that the acidity of the wine would cleanse his wound. He kept some continually in his mouth; and that alone acted so beneficially that he became cured, and I again acquired one more friend.

In this horrible situation we remained six days. Finally, they spoke of capitulating, as by temporizing for so long a time, our retreat had been cut off. A cessation of hostilities took place, and my husband, who was thoroughly worn out, was able for the first time in a long while to lie down upon a bed.

On the 17th of October the capitulation was consummated. Now the good woman who had brought us water at the risk of her life, received the reward of her services. Everyone threw a handful of money into her apron, and she received altogether over twenty guineas. At such a moment the heart seems to be specially susceptible of gratitude.

The Capitulation—Burgoyne Summons Council of War. Burgoyne knowing himself to be surrounded by over-whelming numbers; for the American militia had been pouring in from everywhere since the battles; called a council of war on the 13th, laid the situation before it, and inquired if in its opinion a proposition to surrender would be warranted by precedent, and would it be honorable. The council agreed that surrender was the wisest course. They were doubtless urged to this conclusion by a forceful argument in the shape of a cannon ball that swept across the table about which they were sitting.

Accordingly General Burgoyne sent a flag of truce asking if Gates would receive a "field officer from him, on a matter of high moment to both armies." Gates replied that he would receive such an officer at 10 o'clock the next morning, the 14th. Major Robert Kingston, of Burgoyne's staff, was selected to bear the message to Gates. The next morning at the appointed hour Kingston descended the hill, and, crossing the creek on some sleepers of the bridge that had been left, was met there by Colonel Wilkinson, who represented Gates, and who, after blindfolding him, conducted him on foot down to headquarters, over a mile away.

Burgoyne Sues for an Armistice. Through him Burgoyne asked for a cessation of hostilities while terms might be arranged for an honorable surrender. General Gates sent back the terms on which he would accept the surrender of the British army, and granted a cessation of hostilities during the negotiations. Gates' terms seemed to offend the pride of Burgoyne and his generals, who thereupon refused point blank to treat upon such conditions. The offensive articles were, first: that the British should surrender as prisoners of war; and, second: that they should lay down their arms within their intrenchments at the command of their adjutant general.

At sunset Burgoyne returned Gates' propositions with the answer that he and his army would die to a man rather than submit to conditions involving such humiliation. Along with this answer he presented the terms on which he would consent to a surrender. Gates, evidently frightened by the news just received that Sir Henry Clinton had broken through the obstructions and had passed the forts in the Highlands; that he had destroyed Kingston, and was advancing upon Albany, tamely accepted Burgoyne's proposals, and thus allowed the British general to dictate his own terms.

Terms of Surrender Agreed Upon. But before any treaty could be signed, there were several subordinate questions and items which must be settled; for this purpose two men from each side were selected, at Burgoyne's suggestion, who were to meet at some convenient place, to be selected, to arrange the final terms. A tent was pitched upon the bluff, just south of the Horicon mill, where the representatives met and, after due discussion, signed and exchanged the articles of capitulation, and moreover agreed when they separated, at 8 p.m. of the 15th, that their respective chiefs should sign and exchange in the morning. Burgoyne expressed himself as well pleased with everything, but objected to calling

Passionate depictions were rendered in France, where another revolution was inspired by the American one. *SNHP.*

A short distance from the charred remains, on October 17, 1777, General Schuyler made a gracious gesture in giving shelter from the stress of war and surrender to the German general's wife, Madame von Riedesel and her children. *Lossing.*

the instrument a "treaty of capitulation"; he would term it a treaty of convention. To this also Gates agreed.

During the night of the 15th, a spy managed to get through to the British camp with the news that Clinton was on the way with relief, and was now nearing Albany. Burgoyne saw here a ray of hope, and the next morning called another general council of his officers, told them what he had heard, and asked whether in their opinion he would be justified, under the circumstances, in repudiating his agreement with the American General. The majority decided that the public faith had been pledged, and therefore voted that it would be dishonorable to abrogate the treaty. However, instead of signing the Convention, as he had agreed, he sent Gates an evasive letter, in which he charged him with having reduced his army since negotiations were opened, and asked that two of his officers might be permitted to inspect his army, that he might know if it was as large as reported. Gates was evidently nettled by the rudeness and impudence of the request, but sent Wilkinson to allay Burgoyne's apprehensions.

This parley was spun out to such a length that finally Gates, who had just heard of the burning of Kingston by the British, got impatient, drew up his army, and sent Burgoyne word that he must either sign or fight. Burgoyne, urged by his generals, came down from his perch, on Prospect Hill, signed the Convention and sent it over to Gates in proper form.

And let us never, never, forget that this was wholly an American victory; foreign elements had little or nothing to do with it. With the exception of Gates, a mere figurehead, native born soldiers, led by native born officers, fought all the battles that culminated at Saratoga. For the first time in her history proud old England here surrendered an army, and that to a host of embattled farmers, the sort of men her ruling classes, then and for long, regarded with lordly contempt. A French fleet and a French army helped round up Cornwallis at Yorktown.

The Fate of the Two Armies. The captured army marched south and stayed the first night on their old camp ground at Wilbur's Basin, whence they had been driven ten days before. The next day our people separated the Germans from the British. The British crossed the river on the floating bridge which had been thrown across by Gates at Bemis Heights, and took the old Hoosac road through Northampton, Mass., for Boston. The Germans crossed in boats near Mechanicville, and stayed the next night at Schaghticoke; thence marched south through Troy and Kinderhook to Claverack; thence east through the Berkshires by the way of Springfield to Boston.

Congress did not keep the contract made by Gates to send the surrendered army back to England immediately. The reason for this was that several of the regiments, in defiance of the capitulation, failed to surrender their colors; but which with the military chest were effectually concealed in various ways by the officers. And furthermore, rumors reached Congress, and it was led to believe that the British soldiers meant to break their parole, join Howe's army and renew the fight against us. So they marched them from Boston down to Virginia, thence they were moved hither and yon till after peace was declared.

Washington himself advised Congress to this course. Burgoyne was permitted to return to England, where he received but a cold reception at the hands of the king and people. Afterwards, however, he largely regained his popularity. He died in 1792, and was honored with burial in Westminster Abbey.

Research on the Convention Army continues to turn up new findings.

1929: FRANKLIN D. ROOSEVELT

Governor Franklin D. Roosevelt braved a cold wind to speak before one thousand Rotarians and guests at the Battlefield for the 152nd anniversary of the surrender. He said in the *Saratogian* newspaper on October 18, 1929:

Franklin D. Roosevelt maintained an ongoing interest in the Saratoga Battlefield, honoring it with visits both as governor and as president. This 1996 painting by local artist Judy Vincent depicts his 1940 visit to select the site of the Park's new visitor center, with CCC workers lining the road they had built for him that morning. *Stillwater (NY) Free Library.*

It is national ground. State and nation should work hand in hand in keeping the memory of freedom and liberty alive here. I would have (the Commission) lay out the field as it actually was during the battle, with the trenches and forts and I would have them establish a central point where the layman without a knowledge of the technical strategies of the war could visualize the high points of the battle.

1977: Two Hundred Years On—U.S. Postal Service Commemorative Stamp Ceremonies

From the official program for First Day of Issue ceremonies, "Surrender at Saratoga," October 7, 1977.

The victory had far reaching effects. The surrender of "Gentleman Johnny" and his army not only restored the sagging confidence of the Americans in their own military abilities at a time it was most needed, but brought foreign recognition and aid—assistance that would make the final victory a reality at Yorktown, four years later. All this was made possible by a most remarkable encounter fought on the Heights just south of Saratoga.

But there is more than the military significance, the immediate significance of the time. It is here that every American can stand and truthfully say "had not Gates beaten Burgoyne on this spot, I might not be an American today."

2012: From "Of Gentlemen," by Park Ranger Joe Craig

In the twenty-first century, applications of social analysis come into the telling of eighteenth-century conditions. Here Ranger Joe Craig of Saratoga National Park informs with a playful quiz that was first published in *The Battlements*, the newsletter of Friends of Saratoga Battlefield.

How would you rate as an eighteenth-century gentleman? Take this quiz and find out.

In Their Own Words

1. You are on your way to dinner with a senior officer. You pass a work detail of troops engaged in building fortifications. You:

a. Ignore them.
b. Doff your hat to them.
c. Tell their sergeant that they missed a spot.

2. You are proceeding to your place at the head of your command. A common soldier steps from the ranks and offers you a swig from a proffered jug. You:

a. Take a hearty drink.
b. Ignore him.
c. Have him flogged for speaking out of turn.

3. You have acquired large debts and have taken out a loan from a moneylender. As soon as you get the money, you:

a. Pay off all your creditors.
b. Live a bit more frugally.
c. Re-enact The Rake's Progress.

4. At dinner, a senior officer tells you to sit at the head of the table, normally his place. You:

a. Politely refuse, urging him to take his place.
b. Park your carcass and tuck into dinner.
c. Offer the place of honor to a brother officer.

5. You and a brother officer (whose finances are better than yours) having drunk a bumper to the landlady are about to leave her establishment. You both leave payment, but your brother officer also tosses down a gold guinea [equivalent to twenty-one shillings, a bit more than $100 USD]. You:

a. Decide to let him buy the drinks from now on.
b. Toss your last guinea on the table next to his as money is nothing to a gentleman.
c. Ignore the gesture, you've paid enough for your drink.

6. Another officer speaks disparagingly of the woman about whom you've offered as a toast during dinner. You:

a. Call him out for a early morning's pistols for two and breakfast for one.
b. Jump across the table and beat the chicken soup out of him.
c. Ignore the whelp as he's below your contempt.

7. You've just acquired money for your subsistence, and you learn that the sick and wounded in the hospital are entirely devoid of proper food. You:

a. Head for your quarters and enjoy a good bottle and steak.
b. Bring it to the attention of the chaplain, and he'll alert the higher ups.
c. Give half of your newly acquired money for the relief of the sick and injured.

8. A dangerous assignment needs an officer to command it. You know that the chances of coming out alive are not very good. When the call for volunteers comes, you:

a. Hope that some higher-ranking loony will take it, get killed and leave a vacancy that you can fill.
b. Demand the "honor" to be yours.
c. Go only if you're asked nicely.

Answers (with documentation):

1. b "[The deponent] Also recollects of seeing General Washington twice on the road with his life guard with him and will never forget while he retains his memory the polite bow that the general made to the poor wagoners as he passed them." [Pension claim of William Burnett, submitted 1841.]

2. a "At the time of our engagement at Gov. Penn's castle, Gen. Washington and his aides, Col Meade and Col. Stuart…were riding in front of us when an illbred soldier by the name of John Brantly…who had picked up a jug of wine in the course of the course of the day, seeing

General Washington coming by, dropt his musket and went to meet him saying, 'Won't you drink some wine with a soldier?'

The General said, 'My God, boy, there is no time for drinking wine.'

'God Almighty d--n your proud soul,' says the soldier, 'You are above drinking with soldiers,' on hearing which the general put his chestnut sorrel about suddenly, saying, 'Come I will drink with you.'

Brantly then gave him the jug, which he put to his mouth and handed it back.

'Give it to your servants,' says the soldier, meaning his aides. They all applied it to their lips and returned it. 'Now,' says the soldier, 'I'll be d----d if I don't spend the last drop of my heart's blood for you,' and the general proceeded on his way." [From the memoir of Hugh McDonald, North Carolina Continental Soldier.]

3. c <u>From the School for Scandal</u> [Act IV, Scene 1, Richard Brinsley Sheridan, 1776].
Careless. "…but don't let that old blockhead persuade you to squander any of that money on musty old debts, or any such nonsense; for tradesmen, Charles, are the most exorbitant fellows."
Charles. "Very true, and paying them is only encouraging them."

4. a "If any one far surpasses others, either in age, estate, or merit, yet would give place to one meaner than himself in his own lodging, the one ought not to accept it; so he, on the other hand, should not use much earnestness nor offer it above once or twice." [Rules of Civility & Decent Behavior, #31, as copied by G. Washington at age 14.]

5. b "I had formed an acquaintance with Lord G[uilfor]d, son of a noble Earl, he called on me one evening, in company with a noted attorney…His lordship complained he was very thirsty, and desired I would send for a pot of porter. It was brought and they both drank of it. When they were going Lord G[uilfor]d, threw a guinea on the table, and desired the attorney to put down another. He replied, 'Not indeed, my Lord! I think your guinea is sufficient to pay for fifty pots of porter! What two guineas for a pot of porter! I have not such a fortune as you have, to throw away my guineas in such a way.'—Why M[orgel]l, said my Lord, I thought you would give five guineas for sitting in that lady's [sic] company. But I suppose you have no change about you. Come, come, I'll pay for you—which he did. His lordship went away laughing, and the man of the law scolding, muttering, and grumbling as he went along.

What a contrast between the two. The one sordid and mean, the other noble and generous." Memoirs of Margaret Leeson, 1795. [This worthy individual was also known as Peg Plunkett, whore and procuress. Her memoir was a "high society tell all" for Dublin.]

6. a See Henry Fielding's <u>The History of Tom Jones, A Foundling</u> (1749) Chapters 11–14. Jones opted for a sword, but the effect is the same.

7. c "Our poor sick and wounded lay without medicine and provisions in such pitiable circumstances that the hardest heart had to be moved. Their food consisted of stinking salted meat and some flour or worm-

Ranger Joe Craig reads the Declaration of Independence, a Fourth of July tradition at the Park. *SNHP.*

eaten biscuit…A few hundred guineas could have relieved the misery of these unfortunates, since fresh provisions were brought to market after the surrender. I received thirty guineas on a bill of exchange and gave half to these forsaken men." [Diary of Johann Ewald, Hessian Field Jager Corps, October 1781.]

8.b "We had scarcely arrived in the vicinity of St. Andrew's Church [SC] when we were greeted with cannon shots from the opposite bank of St. Andrew's Creek, whereupon the army halted. Now, since it could cost many men to drive away the enemy and capture the bridge, the general asked me whether I would not attempt to cross a little further up the creek, which would force the enemy to leave his post. If not, cannon must be brought up, since nothing could be accomplished here with four amusettes.

Who would say 'No' if he thinks of distinguishing himself? I accepted the offer." [Diary of Johann Ewald, Hessian Field Jager Corps, March 1780.]

Number of correct answers: 6 or more, a True Gentleman; 5 to 6, needs work, but there's hope; 4 or less, get back to digging ditches.

Chapter 6

A Force for Renewal

CATALYST FOR REGIONAL GROWTH

Reassessing and planning for the future adds vitality within the park and in the region. While park management regularly considers such topics as the park's landscape, visitor use, collections and furnishings, there is a major reassessment undertaken every twenty to thirty years. SNHP underwent this process beginning in 2000 to revise the 1969 master plan. The result was the General Management Plan of 2004.

Park staff, scholars and resource specialists worked to define the park's interpretive themes and how to best engage them for the public. Expert viewpoints were sought in cultural resource management, historic preservation, interpretation, collections management, landscape architecture, history, archaeology and natural resource management. The public was invited to participate at all stages of research.

The resulting consensus was to focus on the park as memorial grounds, to find means to improve visitor understanding with a more complete and logical depiction of the events of 1777 and to expand partnerships with other Burgoyne-related sites and regional entities in the Champlain-Hudson and Mohawk Valleys.

Left: The reenactment experience, a chance to walk in history. *SNHP.*

Below: Continental artillery crew. *SNHP.*

A Force for Renewal

ALLIES AND ALLIANCES

The tradition and meanings of the Saratoga battles inspire organizations, sites and events. The following are highlights of the years leading into the twenty-first century.

1990: Old Saratoga/New Schuylerville Association, a countywide initiative sponsored by the Saratoga County Chamber of Commerce, begins a ten-year campaign with projects small and large for the village of Schuylerville.

1994: Decommissioning of the USS *Saratoga*, Carrier Vessel 60. The $80,000 silver service, donated by area residents sixty-five years earlier, returns home to the Saratoga area.

1997: The Wilkinson Trail on the battlefield is dedicated after ten years in the planning and preparation. Donations and "sweat equity" have come from the region and overseas.

Overlooking the veterans' memorial at Stop 2 at the Battlefield. *SNHP.*

1998: War heroes—recipients of the Congressional Medal of Honor—choose Saratoga for their meeting because of its meaning in American history.

1999: Saratoga National Cemetery is dedicated, joining Arlington and the other national cemeteries prepared to receive veterans and members of military families with honor. Its planned capacity is seventy thousand.

2000: The March for Parks, a fundraiser sponsored by SNHP and the Friends of Saratoga Battlefield, hits its peak. The April event is co-chaired by Charles V. Wait and Christel Maclean. A major contribution will result in production of a new orientation film at the park's Visitor Center.

2001: A fundraiser, the Monument Challenge, is overshadowed by the calamity of 9/11. SNHP receives an unexpected surge in attendance and patriotic expression.

2002: The 225th Anniversary of the Burgoyne campaign and the battles of Saratoga are celebrated on a scale reminiscent of 1877 and 1927. The renovated Saratoga Monument is reopened.

2003–4: The proposals of the Old Saratoga/New Schuylerville Association are bound into a $35 million project package named Schuyler Park and delivered to elected representatives.

2006: A new entity is formed by the New York legislature. The Historic Saratoga–Washington on the Hudson Partnership includes fifteen nongovernmental organizations and fifteen municipalities in the Hudson River Valley.[37]

2010: The Victory Woods is opened for public visitation. It is a unit of SNHP and comprises the acreage surrounding General Burgoyne's camp during his last stand on the heights of Saratoga, October 10–17, 1777.

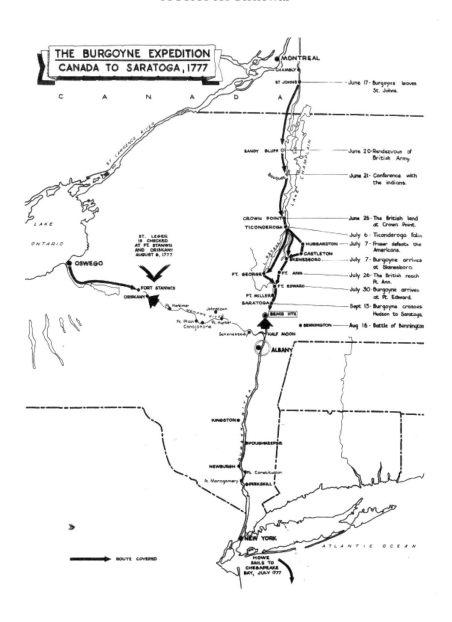

Commemorative events followed the Burgoyne campaign down the Champlain and Hudson Valleys. *Chaucer/Cooper.*

Reenactment crews and regiments were active throughout 2002, the year of the 225th anniversary. *SNHP.*

The Victory Woods trail is accessible and includes interpretive signage. *SNHP.*

2011: The Sword Surrender Site is secured by the Open Space Institute of New York, and plans are designed for its interpretation and accessibility to the public.

The development of the Old Saratoga sites moves to the forefront of planning among regional organizations and municipalities. The engagement with communities continues with school and library programs, and coordination with local business and social organizations grows. The interlacing of community and battlefield activities increases, and programs at the battlefield strengthen through diligence of park personnel even though the budget undergoes reduction.

The robust program of SNHP is seen in its yearly calendar of events at the end of this book.

Realistic living history—the Second New Hampshire after moving back in haste from Hubbardton, where the men left their coats behind on July 7, 1777. *SNHP.*

Personalities of importance to the battles are brought to life here at the Neilson House. *SNHP*

2013: Plans are in the works for celebrating the seventy-fifth anniversary of SNHP.

2015: The battlefield and the battles are honored by preparations for issuance by the United States Mint of a commemorative quarter depicting the surrender of General Burgoyne.

2027: The 250th anniversary of the Burgoyne campaign and the battles of Saratoga inspire discussion among living history and scholarly groups.

HOW FRIENDS GROUPS WORK

In national parks from Acadia in Maine to Hawaii, local residents have organized to contribute to parks in their areas, enhancing parks' effectiveness and the experiences visitors may enjoy.

National Historical Parks are initially established to conserve, interpret and make available special places selected for their significance in American history. Such places are valued for events that happened there and are valued for their part in telling the story of America. NPs of other types include those that contain natural attributes deemed of such value that they deserve to be protected and preserved for generations to come. State park systems are maintained similarly.

Friendly Groups: Leading to the Creation of Parks

As seen earlier in this book, conversations begin spontaneously among enthusiasts recognizing a special purpose. A conversation becomes a committee, and a committee becomes formally organized.

In the case of SNHP, the commitment of memory and expression of honor in the 1850–77 period took form in monument building. The Saratoga Monument was placed on the spot where Burgoyne's command post endured its last hours.

Self-prompted tours were developed by individuals to visit the famous places of battle from this time until the early twentieth century, while the landscape went on, little changing from the agricultural uses that had preceded the battles.

In an era of increasing mobility, considerations of attraction and preservation combined in organizing land ownership and use of the renowned battleground.

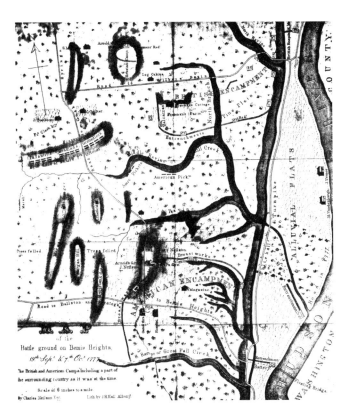

George W. Neilson, a grandson of John Neilson, continued the family farm through the nineteenth century. President of the 1877 celebration of the Saratoga victory at Bemis Heights, he sponsored a map for tours of the Battlefield. *SSHM.*

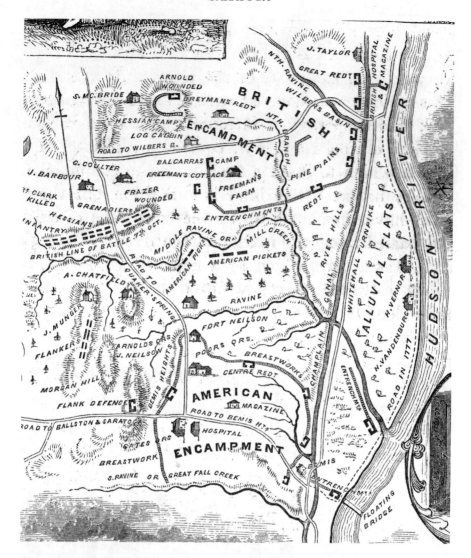

Ellen Hardin Walworth's map for visitors to the Battlefield used for georeferences the roads of 1877. *Lossing.*

As Franklin D. Roosevelt moved through the ranks from governor to president and carried along with him his care and concern for the Saratoga Battlefield, his interest was paralleled by many in the region. Events such as the pageants in 1911, 1912, 1926 and 1927 were wildly popular. Local parades and fetes were perennially enjoyed in nearby communities.

When New York State and the United States took the battlefield into their parks systems, the small core of paid personnel was mirrored by enthusiasts and volunteers in the towns and counties around the Saratoga area. As of 2012, paid staff at SNHP numbered fewer than twenty and were able to maintain the three-thousand-acre park and maximize their effectiveness by working with about sixty trained volunteers and hundreds of members of organizations dedicated to the themes SNHP represents. Affiliations meet in the extraordinary experiences available at the park with annual events observed by groups such as the Daughters of the American Revolution, Sons of the American Revolution and Children of the American Revolution.

The Old Saratoga Historical Association grew from the Historical Publicity Committee formed in 1949 by representatives of several community organizations "to encourage historical recognition of this [Schuylerville] community." One of the initial activities of this committee was to work to change the name of the village of Schuylerville to "Saratoga" or "Old Saratoga." Other ventures included holding historical appreciation week, staffing an information booth, sponsoring Surrender Day, organizing radio and television programs to commemorate the 175th anniversary of the battles of Saratoga, writing weekly newspaper columns on the early history of Saratoga County and offering historical tours of the area.

In 1952, the Old Saratoga Historical Association of Schuylerville, New York, Inc., was established for the purposes of disseminating information concerning historic events and places, both national and state, and for the discovery, procurement and preservation of historic relics and places relating to the state of New York in the pre-Revolutionary and Revolutionary periods, with particular reference to the preservation and development of the scenes of the decisive battles of Saratoga. The association has been involved in procuring furnishings for the Philip Schuyler House, staffing and giving tours of the house and promoting the site, the Saratoga Monument and the Saratoga Battlefield.

The two biggest events hosted by the group for many years have been the annual 18th Century Day, held at the Philip Schuyler House in August to help visitors learn about life and artisans in the eighteenth century, and the Candlelight Tour of the Schuyler House, held in mid-October each year, when guests see the house by candlelight and learn about

The Old Saratoga Historical Association works with the Park to maintain accuracy of the furnishings in the Schuyler House, bringing close the authenticity of experience for the annual Candlelight Tour in October. *SNHP.*

the Schuyler family and their home. OSHA presents many program meetings each year: a book read with a subject touching on the life of early Schuylerville-area inhabitants, field trips to nearby local history sites and sessions when members reflect on life in days gone by. A recent gathering discussed personal recollections of one-room schoolhouse days. The group offers scholarships to Schuylerville High School students and produces a calendar with pictures from the local historian or members.

An ad hoc group, United Saratoga Associates, in 1984 followed up the Saratoga NHP acquisition of the Saratoga Monument with a proposal to rehabilitate the Saratoga Monument and to revitalize the national park, nearby villages and surrounding areas.

The spark that prompted action was the response of a visitor from abroad who was shocked by the neglect given to sacred places of the national story.

The USA proposition was that with the prospect of a new era in telecommunications and wider understanding of regional effects of

Volunteer hosts of the popular living history experiences are perpetual students of their subjects and craft. *T. Holmes.*

great events, a regional approach could be taken in public and private sectors to shape Saratoga   destinations. A "kitchen cabinet" of local entrepreneurs working toward renovation of Schuylerville developed the discussion. Such concepts were styled as the "Gettysburg of the Revolution" and "the Williamsburg of the North East."[38]

The superintendent of the park engaged in the dialogue. By 1989, alignment with policies on the United States Department of the Interior and the NPS gave rise to the proposal for a Friends group.

The Friends of Saratoga Battlefield was chartered under the State University of New York Education Department on July 27, 1990. Among its purposes was to stimulate interest in the history of the Saratoga National Historical Park, which includes the battlefield, the Schuyler House, Victory Woods and the Saratoga Monument; to be

With the Northern Army
The 20ᵗʰ Day of Sep. 09

Pafs The Bearer:
Cathe Woodward
Through Our Lines EnRoute to:
Springs at Saratoga
Lt. Ambrose Maw

A Continental army
reenactor grants a
visitor a safe conduct
pass, which would
allow a member of an
enemy army (in this
case, the British or their
mercenaries) to pass
through American-held
territory without fear
of harassment, bodily
harm or death. *SNHP.*

an advocate on behalf of the Saratoga National Historical Park; to
generate appreciation of its heritage and history; and to provide a
common meeting ground for those who are interested in the Saratoga
National Historical Park.

The group set about raising a membership base and fundraising.
For this the leadership conceived events tied to the battlefield and the
battlefield story.

Among those who were immediately drawn to the purpose were
teachers, farmers, former IBM executives, emergency squad workers,
a yacht basin owner and a retired lieutenant colonel from the U.S. Air
Force Strategic Air Command. War veterans and those dedicated to

A Force for Renewal

During the Revolutionary War, and especially for the British army, women provided such essential services as laundering and mending clothing, cooking meals and nursing the wounded. On the march, these "camp followers," who may have been wives or mistresses, were expected to keep up, often carrying pots and pans, personal belongings and children as they struggled to keep pace. *SNHP.*

It took a well-trained crew to coordinate the actions required for a successful cannon shot. Duties included moving the cannon carriages into position, setting the fuse and loading and firing the weapon, tasks still performed in today's army but with modern technology. *SNHP.*

remembrance of the country's foundation were especially interested in becoming active. A solid membership base was established by consistently presenting engaging programs true to the organization's purpose.

In its first twenty years, the Friends of Saratoga Battlefield participated in many of the events that engaged the community. The annual March for Parks series was driven by the objective of raising funds for the orientation film now shown daily at the SNHP Visitor Center. With raising awareness a priority, the Friends hosted a premiere of a recent public television service series on the national parks by the documentary filmmaker Ken Burns.

Living history is a part of the volunteer life brought to the Saratoga Battlefield. This incorporates historical tools, activities and dress into an interactive presentation that gives observers and participants a sense of stepping back in time. Although it does not always seek to reenact a specific event in history, living history is similar to, and sometimes incorporates, historical reenactment such as the massing of many reenactor regiments on the occasion of the 225th anniversary of Burgoyne's defeat.

SANCTUARY OF POWER

On the morning of 9/11, 2001, the world changed for many Americans as the World Trade Center towers came down. For those on the scene, it was a time for action: to find safety, to assist in rescue and to search for the lost. For those observing the tragedy unfold from distant points in the United States and elsewhere, the changing feelings of disbelief, shock and anger swept over.

At the Saratoga Battlefield, it was an extraordinary day. An unexpectedly large crowd came to the park ("once a scene of war, now a place of peace"). There were no events planned that day. Those who came shared their astonishment, grief and dismay with park personnel and strangers, friends they had not met before. For the rangers on duty and visitors alike, it was a day of revelation. The sense of the long-ago victory, unexpected and against all odds, filled those present with confidence, hope and strength.

As an appropriate ending, here are some authentic eighteenth-century toasts, as offered (in lemonade) by Ranger Joe Craig at the annual Fourth of July citizenship ceremony at the Saratoga Battlefield:

> *To the Memory of the Brave Offices and Men who have Fallen in Defense of American Liberty!*
> *George Rejected and Liberty Protected!*
> *To those who wish America ill, may they enjoy perpetual itching without scratching!*
> *Liberty to those who have Spirit to Assert it!*
> Huzzah!

Saratoga National Historical Park Interpretive Themes

Saratoga National Historical Park opened the twenty-first century by committing to these themes.

SNHP PRIMARY INTERPRETIVE THEMES

Primary interpretive themes are those ideas or concepts that every visitor to a park should understand. They are the key ideas through which the park's nationally significant resource meanings are conveyed to the public. These themes provide the foundation for interpretive programs and media at the park. The themes do not include everything we may wish to interpret but rather the ideas that are critical to a visitor's understanding of the park's significance. *All interpretive efforts, including talks and tours, should relate to one or more of the interpretive themes and should guide the formation and execution of the overall interpretive program.*

SNHP FINAL INTERPRETIVE THEMES, APRIL 2001

At Saratoga, the British campaign that was supposed to crush America's
rebellion ended instead in a surrender that changed the history of the world.
—Richard Ketchum

Place: Grand Strategy and Victory for the New Nation

In 1777—the second year of America's War for Independence—the British sought to quell the open rebellion with a single decisive military campaign. Their plan depended on using an invading army to divide the colonies along a natural corridor of rivers and lakes stretching from Canada to New York City. The American commitment to halt this invasion at Saratoga proved critical to the future of an emerging nation.

The Americans' determined resistance at Saratoga, coupled with British strategic blunders, resulted in a stunning defeat and surrender for a British army. This timely victory reversed American military fortunes, boosted patriot morale and gained them international recognition and support, including vital naval and military assistance.

The defensive position south of Saratoga at Bemis Heights was chosen because the natural terrain features there afforded the Americans tactical advantages. Their skillful use of the high ground, narrow river passageway and wooded ravines, fortified with entrenchments and batteries, forced the advancing British army to fight the battles on terms favorable to the Americans.

Since pre-colonial times, the waterways of the Hudson and Mohawk Rivers and Lakes Champlain and George had been prized natural routes of communication, trade and warfare—highly coveted by those seeking control of this vast inland area and its rich natural resources and arable land.

People: At Saratoga, by Choice or by Chance

Today, the winning of American independence seems to have been inevitable. But it was actually the result of many individual decisions and sacrifices made by real people from all walks of life and of all political persuasions. Their determination in surmounting enormous obstacles was an early example of what is recognized now as the American spirit—the will and ability to shape a better future.

Participants on both sides of the conflict—men and women, soldiers and civilians, free or enslaved and of those of many nations—were motivated by hopes and aspirations, including reasons of personal or monetary gain, continuance of established ways of life, desire for a better future or their belief in a moral cause.

General Philip Schuyler, a patriot statesman and military leader, risked his life and livelihood and lost his Saratoga home for his belief in the promise of a new and independent United States of America, affording political and economic liberties for its citizens. After his death, his family continued his policies of promoting canal transportation and fostering commercial enterprise in the community that became known as Schuylerville in his honor.

Memory: Creating a Shared American Identity

Monuments and memorials added to Saratoga's "sacred ground" represent early national efforts to honor those who served their country and the causes for which they made their sacrifices. The park and its monuments and historic markers contribute to a shared American identity and an evolving sense of patriotism.

The Saratoga Monument stands prominently within the British camp where the decision to surrender was made in October 1777. The site symbolizes the decisive turn in the American struggle for independence and serves as an eternal reminder of the human cost of both the American victory and the British defeat.

Ellen Hardin Walworth's efforts to commemorate the Saratoga battles marked the beginning of her lifelong commitment to preserving the icons of our national identity and the creation of local, state and national organizations to achieve those goals.

Articles of Convention Between Lieutenant General Burgoyne and Major General Gates

I. The troops under Lieutenant-General Burgoyne, to march out of their camp with the honors of war, and the artillery of the intrenchments, to the verge of the river where the old fort stood, where the arms and artillery are to be left; the arms are to be piled by word of command from their own officers.

II. A free passage to be granted to the army under Lieutenant-General Burgoyne to Great Britain, on condition of not serving again in North America during the present contest; and the port of Boston is assigned for the entry of transports to receive the troops whenever General Howe shall so order.

III. Should any cartel take place, by which the army under General Burgoyne, or any part of it, may be exchanged, the foregoing article to be void as far as such exchange shall be made.

IV. The army under Lieutenant-General Burgoyne, to march to Massachusetts Bay, by the easiest, most expeditious and convenient route; and to be quartered in, near, or as convenient as possible to Boston, that the march of the troops may not be delayed when transports arrive to receive them.

V. The troops to be supplied on their march, and during their being in quarters, with provisions by General Gates' orders at the same rate of rations as the troops of his own army; and if possible, the officers' horses and cattle are to be supplied with forage at the usual rates.

VI. All officers to retain their carriages, batt-horses and other cattle, and no baggage to be molested or searched; Lieutenant-General Burgoyne giving his honor that there are no public stores secreted therein. Major-General Gates will, of course, take the necessary measures for the due performance of this article. Should any carriages be wanted during the march for the transportation of officers' baggage, they are, if possible, to be supplied by the country at the usual rates.

VII. Upon the march, and during the time the army shall remain in quarters in Massachusetts Bay, the officers are not, as far as circumstances will admit, to be separated from their men. The officers are to be quartered according to rank, and are not to be hindered from assembling their men for roll call, and other necessary purposes of regularity.

VIII. All corps whatever, of General Burgoyne's army, whether composed of sailors, bateaumen, artificers, drivers, independent companies, and followers of the army, of whatever country, shall be included in the fullest sense and utmost extent of the above articles, and comprehended in every respect as British subjects.

IX. All Canadians and persons belonging to the Canadian establishment, consisting of sailors, bateaumen, artificers, drivers, independent companies, and many other followers of the army, who come under no particular description, are to be permitted to return there; they are to be conducted immediately by the shortest route to the first British post on Lake George, are to be supplied with provisions in the same manner as the other troops, and are to be bound by the same condition of not serving during the present contest in North America.

X. Passports to be immediately granted for three officers, not exceeding the rank of captain, who shall be appointed by Lieutenant-General Burgoyne, to carry dispatches to Sir William Howe, Sir Guy Carleton, and to Great Britain, by the way of New York; and Major-General Gates engages the public faith, that these despatches shall not be opened. These officers are to set out immediately after receiving their despatches, and are to travel the shortest and in the most expeditious manner.

XI. During the stay of the troops in Massachusetts Bay the officers are to be admitted on parole, and are to be allowed to wear their side arms.

XII. Should the army under Lieutenant-General Burgoyne find it necessary to send for their clothing and other baggage to Canada, they are to be permitted to do it in the most convenient manner, and the necessary passports granted for that purpose.

XIII. These articles are to be mutually signed and exchanged tomorrow morning at nine o'clock, and the troops under Lieutenant-General Burgoyne are to march out of their intrenchments at three o'clock in the afternoon.

(Signed) HORATIO GATES, Major-General.
(Signed) J. BURGOYNE, Lieutenant-General.

Saratoga, Oct. 16th, 1777.

Appendix III

Fate of a Trophy of the Burgoyne Campaign

Ogdensburg, New York, February 22, 1813

WAR OF 1812

Narrative of Lou Myers, living history interpreter, Saratoga, February 2012, and http://www.1000islands.com/ogdensburg/war_1812.

British forces had crossed the ice from Prescott on the Canadian side of the St. Lawrence River and approached Ogdensburg.

Captain Giles Kellogg's Company of Artillery, about seventy men from Schoharie County, commanded their one cannon, an iron twelve-pounder mounted on a wheel carriage that had been taken from Burgoyne at Saratoga. The cannon had been a trophy from the Revolutionary War. Kellogg and his men had been sent to Ogdensburg in late December to help protect and defend the inhabitants of the northern frontier. As the British approached, Kellogg fired his cannon, but the elevation screw broke on the first shot, rendering it useless. Kellogg and his men withdrew, heading over the bridge to join Captain Benjamin Forsyth's rifle regiment at the fort on the west side of the Oswegatchie.

Leaving their coats and all else with the now defunct relic of the Burgoyne campaign, the company was defeated with a loss of everything, except the clothing they had on and the small arms with which they fought.

A bronze smoothbore, muzzle-loading 5.75-caliber howitzer is thirty-three inches long and weighs 468 pounds. It was made in England by R. Gilpin in 1760 and is engraved with the marks of the master general of the Royal Ordnance. After the British defeat at Saratoga, this piece and thirty-four other cannons were additionally inscribed with "Surrendered by the Convention of Saratoga, October 17, 1777." *Libby Holmes.*

The howitzer resided for many decades at the Watervliet Arsenal near Albany, then was transferred in 1900 to the Department of State's Army and Navy building in Washington, D.C. There it remained on display until the early years of World War II when it was rescued from a fate as metal scrap by the personal intervention of President Franklin Roosevelt. The secretary of war released this and other historic trophy ordnance to their respective national military parks. The cannon was returned to Saratoga in 1943, the fifth accession to the collections of the fledgling park.—SNHP info

How Would I Research My Revolutionary War Ancestor?

I. If You Know Name and Unit
II. If You Are Searching to Determine If You Have a Revolutionary War Ancestor

I. If you know a name and unit, the primary source is the National Archives and Records Administration (NARA):
    A. paylists and muster rolls
    B. pension records

    How to get them:
    1. visit a NARA location
    2. commission NARA to conduct a search

Visit NARA's website for specific information: http://www.archives.gov/research_room/obtain_copies/veterans_service_records.html.

II. If you are searching to determine if you have a Revolutionary War ancestor, first conduct an orderly genealogical search. If you find an ancestor apparently with Revolutionary War participation, there will be state records close by to check. States have comprehensive transcriptions of records dating from the 1900 period—for example, in New York State, *New York in the Revolution as Colony and State*; in Massachusetts, *Soldiers and Sailors of the Revolutionary War*; and for Connecticut, the

Record of Connecticut Men in the Military and Naval Service During the War of the Revolution.

The best secondary sources are the Daughters of the American Revolution and the Sons of the American Revolution. These organizations' records are constituted of proving paperwork of generations of applicants. These might provide already completed searches that may be applicable to new researchers.

It is recommended when finalizing research to always get to original resources or good images of them. Microfilm is a widely applied medium. Even transcriptions can be faulty.

How would I learn if my Revolutionary War ancestor was at Saratoga?
A valuable start is at http://saratoganygenweb.com, the database developed by Heritage Hunters, the genealogical association of Saratoga County.

Also useful for overall genealogical research are online services such as fold3.com, available by subscription, and HeritageQuest, which is available to cardholders at many local libraries. HeritageQuest has Revolutionary War pension records and U.S. Census records available to view. Some initial progress can be made in free databases such as Rootsweb, which is hosted by the notable subscription service Ancestry.com.

Fourth of July at Saratoga Battlefield

It has become a Fourth of July tradition at the Saratoga Battlefield for the United States Immigration and Naturalization Service to conduct the induction ceremony for twenty persons becoming American citizens at the site.

Heard from more than one on this occasion: "This is the best day of my life."

Heard from one of the speakers:

> *Once a scene of war, now a place of peace. Years ago, in the wide spaces of this park a rough army—mostly of volunteers, many plain farmers—defeated a British army. It was an unexpected victory and a turning point in the American Revolution. A lasting lesson was the role of* citizen soldiers in changing it all. *This lesson is duplicated today all over the world for the sake of democracy.*
>
> *The battle won here gave hope for the American Revolution, which did succeed, and established a country of many freedoms and possibilities. The rights and freedoms for which they fought have been preserved for you to enjoy as American citizens. Again and again, individual citizens have stepped up to express themselves, to stand for what they believe and to defend what is precious to them.*
>
> *Now you take hold of the privilege, and the power, to contribute freely in American society. We bid that you use this with care and with*

An image from the Saratoga National Historic Park.

wisdom. Thank you for joining us as Americans. We sincerely wish you well, going forward from this time and place, to love, cherish and defend your newfound freedoms.

Notes

CHAPTER 1

1. In respected venues of the study of history, a debate among historians about changes in history ranged between "events, or the flow of events," and "great men." A factor that emerges over time is that of place.
2. *Papers Relating to the Administration of Lieut. Gov. Leisler 1689–1691*, the Documentary History of the State of New York, arranged under direction of Secretary of State Christopher Morgan, by E.B. O'Callaghan, MD, Vol. 2, Albany (1849).
3. Ibid.
4. Jacob Leisler, self-proclaimed lieutenant governor as of June 1689, would himself fall to the forces of political competition and intrigue. Having seized power in the name of King William to replace the "Romish administration" that functioned under James II, he was arrested and hanged for treason in May 1691 by political rivals. He had organized perhaps the first intercolonial military action independent of British authority. He was pardoned posthumously by Parliament.

CHAPTER 2

5. Quoted in Luzader, *Decision on the Hudson.* Endnotes in the 2002 edition are useful sources for details that follow.
6. Ketchum, *Saratoga,* 297–305, 309–328; Luzader, *Decision on the Hudson,* 30–32; Wood, *Battles of the Revolutionary War,* 146–49.
7. Wood, *Battles of the Revolutionary War,* 150.
8 Ketchum, *Saratoga,* 376–78.
9. NPS website and brochures.

CHAPTER 3

10. Stone, *History of the Saratoga Monument Association.*
11. DAR Yearbooks, Saratoga Springs History Museum Archives.
12. *Historical Pageants,* Adoption of the Declaration of Independence and the Surrender of Burgoyne, Schuylerville, New York, July 4, 5, 6 and 7, 1926 program book, authors' collection.
13. *The One Hundred and Fiftieth Anniversary Battles of Saratoga and Surrender of Burgoyne on the Battlefield October 8, 1927,* program book, authors' collection.
14. Private communication.

CHAPTER 4

15. Hal Sheehan, "Over Mechanicville Way," *Schenectady Gazette,* September 14, 1985.
16. *Saratogian,* October 18, 1929.
17. Andrew Tweedie, personal account, copyright 1975, Saratoga Springs Public Library, Saratoga Room files.
18. Memoranda, SNHP Archives.
19. Documents of St. Stephen's Episcopal Church, 1 Grove Street, Schuylerville, New York.
20. Phillips, *Historic Structure Report: General Philip Schuyler House,* vol. 2, 352.

CHAPTER 5

21. *Hadden's Journal*, 314. It took thirty carts to transport Burgoyne's personal baggage. No other officer in the army was allowed a single cart for his private use after they left Fort Edward. All note citations from this extracted sources chapter are as written in Brandow's *Story of Old Saratoga*.
22. *Sparks' American Biography*, vol. 13, 260.
23. *Hadden's Journal*, 81. There were more than three hundred women connected with Burgoyne's army.
24. Major Ackland was a gallant officer and a generous foe. While in New York on parole, he did all in his power to mitigate the treatment of distinguished American prisoners. After his return to England, he sacrificed his life in defense of American honor. At a dinner of military men, the courage of Americans generally was questioned. He repelled the imputation with great energy. High words ensued, during the course of which the lie was passed between him and a subordinate officer named Lloyd. A duel was the consequence, in which the major was killed. As a result, Lady Harriet lost her senses and continued deranged for two years.
25. *Digby's Journal*, 297.
26. Describing her experience in getting started from home, Frau von Riedesel wrote: "Not only did the people tell me of the dangers of the sea, but they also said that we must take care not to be eaten by the savages; and that the people of America lived on horseflesh and cats. But all this frightened me less than the thought of going to a land where I did not understand the language. However, I made up my mind to everything, and the idea of following my husband and doing my duty, held me up through the whole course of my journey." In these days, that would be equal to a wife following her husband on a military expedition into the heart of Africa. The baroness became the mother of nine children.
27. Mr. Hiram Clark of Clark's Mills told the author that he could remember the remnants of that work. It consisted of two lengths of heavy timbers, locked together at one end, placed at an obtuse angle and filled in with dirt behind.
28. W.L. Stone's *Burgoyne's Campaign*, 376.

29. *Wilkinson's Memoirs*, vol. 1.
30. This Captain Nathan Goodale was one of the most efficient of Gates's scouts. He gave Gates the first reliable information concerning the situation of Burgoyne's army during its advance as it lay along the river opposite and above Saratoga. Before the surrender of the British army, no less than 121 prisoners fell into his hands. In 1899, a descendant of Captain Goodale erected a tablet to his memory on Prospect Hill, near the monument. He was killed by Indians in Ohio in 1790.
31. See Baroness Riedesel's account, which immediately follows.
32. *Burgoyne's State of the Expedition*, 1780 edition, 55.
33. *Digby's Journal*, 304.
34. This was from Furnival's battery, north of the Battenkill.
35. This was from Fellows's battery, opposite Schuylerville and south of the Battenkill. Furnival's battery had been ordered to Fort Edward.
36. Seventy soldiers brought their wives with them also.

CHAPTER 6

37. From the Historic Saratoga–Washington on the Hudson Partnership (www.upperhudsonpartnership.org): "In recent years, municipalities and non-profit organizations along the Upper Hudson River have independently initiated local projects that foster the areas' rich natural and cultural heritage, as well as provide for sustainable economic growth. The Historic Saratoga–Washington on the Hudson Partnership was established through an act of legislation in 2006 initiated by Assemblymembers Roy McDonald and Steven Englebright and supported by Senator Joe Bruno to comprehensively support the local efforts through an innovative and voluntary framework of public and private groups, including local and state government. Municipalities may opt into the partnership at any time through a local resolution. PARTNERSHIP MISSION. The Partnership's mission is to preserve, enhance and develop the historic, agricultural, scenic, natural and recreational resources and the significant waterways within the Partnership region. Through the tradition of municipal home rule, the Partnership will foster

collaborative projects with pertinent non-profit and governmental entities with an emphasis on both agricultural and open space protection, economic and tourism development, and the protection and interpretation of our natural and cultural heritage. WIDESPREAD SUPPORT. The Partnership has received enthusiastic support from both local government and non-profit groups within the Upper Hudson Corridor and is meeting monthly to discuss projects, create resolutions in support of like-minded issues, and generally foster its mission to preserve, enhance and develop the historic, agricultural, scenic, natural and recreational resources of the Partnership region. Within 60 months the Partnership has attracted over 4 million dollars in funds for community improvement and equally stimulated private investment."

38. One of the founders was Viola Ilma. The daughter of an operatic personality of the early twentieth century, her activism for youth in the 1930s gained the notice of Eleanor Roosevelt. Her subsequent acquaintance with FDR prefigured her involvement with FDR's esteemed battlefield.

Bibliography

Adams, Charles Francis, ed. *Memoirs of John Quincy Adams, Comprising Portions of His Diary from 1795 to 1848*. Vol. 8. Philadelphia, PA: J.B. Lippincott & Company, 1876.

Advisory Council on Historic Preservation (ACHP). *The Proposed Niagara Mohawk Corporation Easton Nuclear Generating Power Station*. Report on file, Saratoga National Historical Park, Stillwater, New York, 1968.

Albright, Horace M. *Origin of National Park Service Administration of Historic Sites*. Philadelphia, PA: Eastern Parks and Monument Association, 1971. National Park Service Online Book. Retrieved November 17, 2009, from http://www.nps.gov/history/history/online_books/ albright/index.htm.

Allaback, Sarah. *Mission 66 Visitor Centers: The History of a Building Type*, 2000. National Park Service Online Book. Retrieved October 2010 from http:// www.nps.gov/history/history/online_books/allaback/index.htm.

American Scenic and Historic Preservation Society. *Thirteenth Annual Report, 1908, of the American Scenic and Historic Preservation Society to the Legislature of the State of New York*. Albany, NY: J.B. Lyon Company, State Printers, 1908.

Arter, Steve. "Compatriot Charles E. Ogden Leads the Fight to Save the Saratoga Battlefield." *Empire Patriot* 12, no. 1 (Winter 2010). Newsletter of the Empire State Society, Sons of the American Revolution.

Authority of the State of New York. *Laws of the State of New York in Relation to the Erie and Champlain Canals Together with the Annual Reports of the Canal Commissioner*. Albany, NY: self-published, 1825.

Baker, Thomas E. *Redeemed from Oblivion: An Administrative History of Guilford Courthouse National Military Park*. Washington, D.C.: National Park Service, U.S. Department of the Interior, 1995. Online version retrieved on March 23, 2010, from http://*www*.nps.gov/archive/guco/adhi/adhi.htm.

Beach, Allen C. *The Centennial Celebrations of the State of New York*. Albany, NY: Weed, Parsons & Company, 1879.

Bennington Battle Monument Association. *Record History and Description of the Bennington Battle Monument and the Ceremonies at the Lay of the Cornerstone, August 16th, 1887*. Bennington, VT: C.A. Pierce, 1887.

Bennington Historical Society. *The Bennington Battle Monument and Centennial Celebration*. Milford, MA: Cook and Sons, 1877.

Blasdel, R.A., J.Y. Shimoda and I.J. Ellsworth. *Master Plan for the Preservation and Use of Saratoga National Historical Park*. Vol. 3, General Park Information, Section A, Park Origin. Stillwater, NY: Saratoga National Historic Park, 1963.

Bodnar, John. *Remaking America, Public Memory, Commemoration, and Patriotism in the Twentieth Century*. Princeton, NJ: Princeton University Press, 1993.

Brandow, John Henry. *The Story of Old Saratoga*. Albany, NY: Fort Orange Press, Brandow Printing Company, 1919.

Brown, Sylvie C. *Final Report on the 1985 Excavations in the Old Woods, Saratoga Battlefield: The Archeology of a Small Campsite*. Report on file, Saratoga National Historical Park, Stillwater, New York, 1987.

Bryan, John M. *Robert Mills: America's First Architect*. Princeton, NJ: Princeton Architectural Press, 2001.

Campbell, J. Duncan. *Archeological Investigation, Freeman Farm House Site, Saratoga National Historical Park, 9–16 September, 1963*. Report on file, Saratoga National Historical Park, Stillwater, New York, 1963.

Carr, Ethan. *Mission 66: Modernism and the National Park Dilemma*. Amherst: University of Massachusetts Press, 2007.

Committee on Military Affairs. "Cannon to the Saratoga Monument Association." Report to Accompany Bill H.R. 5377. 47th Congress, 1st Session, Report No. 1076. *Index to the Reports of the Committees of the House of Representatives for the First Session of the Forty-Seventh Congress, 1881–1882*. 6 vols. Washington, D.C.: Government Printing Office, 1882.

Cotter, John L. *Archeological Observations, Tenant House Foundations, Schuyler House Grounds*, 1964, Saratoga National Historical Park. Report on file, Northeast Museum Services Center, Charlestown Navy Yard, Charlestown, Massachusetts.

————. *Freeman Farm—Balcarres Redoubt Preliminary Tests*, June 15–29, 1960. Report on file, Saratoga National Historical Park, Stillwater, New York.

————. *Preliminary Archaeological Observations at the Schuyler House and Grounds, Saratoga National Historical Park, Schuylerville, Saratoga, New York*, 1958. Report on file, Northeast Museum Services Center, Charlestown Navy Yard, Charlestown, Massachusetts.

————. *Report on Archeological Work Observed and Conducted at Saratoga NHP by Regional Archeologist*, July 24–31, 1958. Report on file, Saratoga National Historical Park, Stillwater, New York.

————. *Results of Archeological Tests, the Neilson House Location and American RiverLines, Saratoga National Historical Park*. Report on file, Saratoga National Historical Park, Stillwater, New York, 1957.

Cotter, John L., and Jackson W. Moore Jr. *Report of Schuyler House Archeological Investigations, July 22–29, 1958*. Report on file, Saratoga National Historical Park, Stillwater, New York.

Crandall, C.H. "Where Burgoyne Surrendered: The Saratoga Monument." *American Magazine* 8, New Series vol. 3 (May to October 1888): 415–30.

Creasy, Sir Edward Shepherd. *The Fifteen Decisive Battles of the World: From Marathon to Waterloo*. London: Richard Bentley & Son, 1851, 30th edition, 1880.

Curran, Brian A., Anthony Grafton, Pamela O. Long and Benjamin Weiss. *Obelisk: A History*. Cambridge, MA: MIT Press, 2009.

Demers, Paul A., and David R. Starbuck. *Archeological Investigation of the Taylor House Site, Saratoga National Historical Park, Stillwater, New York, June–July 1987*, 1989. Report on file, Saratoga National Historical Park, Stillwater, New York.

Dilsaver, Lary M., ed. *America's National Park System: The Critical Documents*, 1994. National Park Service Online Book. Retrieved November 17, 2009, from http://www.nps.gov/history/history/online_books/anps/index.htm.

Doyle, Joseph B. *20th Century History of Steubenville and Jefferson County, Ohio, and Representative Citizens*. Chicago: Richmond-Arnold Publishing Company, 1910.

Dreiser, Theodore. "America's Sculptors." *New York Times*, September 25, 1898.

Dubois, Muriel. *The Washington Monument*. Mankato, MN: Capstone Press, 2002.

Ehrich, Robert W. *Progress Report on the Archeological Program of Saratoga National Historical Park*, 1941. Report on file, Saratoga National Historical Park, Stillwater, New York.

Encyclopedia Britannica. Eleventh Edition. London: University of Cambridge, 1911.

Finan, Joe, Paul Okey, Tricia Shaw, Dave Mathis, James Hughes Robillard and Patrick Burch. *Champlain Canal Assessment Project, April–August 1995*. Report on file, Saratoga National Historical Park, Stillwater, New York.

Fine, Gary Alan. *Difficult Reputations: Collective Memories of the Evil, Inept, and Controversial*. Chicago: University of Chicago Press, 2001.

French, C. Madrid. "Mission 66: Modern Architecture in the National Parks." Retrieved May 16, 2010, from http://www.mission66.com/mission.html.

Funk, Robert E. *Recent Contributions to Hudson Valley Prehistory*. New York State Museum Memoir 22, Albany, New York, 1976.

Gerlach, Don. *Philip Schuyler and the Growth of New York, 1733–1804*. Office of State History, Albany, New York. Retrieved August 22, 2009, from http://threerivershms.com/schuyler.htm.

Hartgen Archeological Associates Inc. (HAA). *Archeological Identification Study*. Volume 2, *Victory Woods, Village of Victory, Saratoga County, New York*. Submitted to the LA Group, Saratoga Springs, New York, 2006.

————. *Phase IB Archeological Reconnaissance, Saratoga Monument Sewer, Village of Victory, Town of Saratoga, Saratoga County, New York*, 2005. Report on file, Saratoga National Historical Park, Stillwater, New York.

Harvey, Frederick L. *History of the Washington National Monument and of the Washington National Monument Association*. Washington, D.C.: Norman T. Elliot Printing, 1902.

Heitert, Kristen, and Jennifer Banister. *Section 106 Archeological Investigations in Victory Woods for Trail and Boardwalk Creation and Archeological Disturbance Assessment, Battlefield Tour Road Emergency Repair Work, Saratoga National Historical Park, Village of Victory and Stillwater, Saratoga County, New York.*

PAL Report No. 2129. Submitted to the National Park Service, Saratoga National Historical Park, Stillwater, New York, 2007.

Heitert, Kristen, and Matthew Kierstead. *Summary Report, 911 Main Street, Wilmington, Massachusetts, Existing Conditions Documentation*. PAL Report No. 1714. Submitted to Robert Autenzio, Wilmington, Massachusetts.

Hill, Henry Wayland. *An Historical Review of Waterways and Canal Construction in New York State*. Buffalo, NY: Buffalo Historical Society, 1908.

The Historical Marker Database. Retrieved May 23, 2010, from http://www.hmdb.org.

Historic Vermont. "Bennington Battle Monument." Retrieved May 23, 2010, from www.historicvermont.org/bennington.

Holden, James A. *Proceedings of the New York State Historical Association*. Newburgh: New York Historical Association, Newburgh Printers, 1904.

Howe, Dennis E. *The 1985 Magnetometer Survey. In Saratoga National Historical Park, Archeological Progress Report*. In *Saratoga National Historical Park Archeology Progress Report*. Edited by David R. Starbuck. N.p., 1986. Report on file, Saratoga National Historical Park, Stillwater, New York.

Johnson, Eric S. *Archeological Overview and Assessment of the Saratoga National Historical Park, New York* (draft), 1997. Report on file, Saratoga National Historical Park, Stillwater, New York.

Johnson, Rossiter, and John Howard Brown, eds. *The Twentieth Century Biographical Dictionary of Notable Americans*. Vols. 3 and 7. Boston, MA: Biographical Society, 1904.

Ketchum, Richard E. *Saratoga: Turning Point of America's Revolutionary War*. New York: John McCrea/Henry Holt Publishing Company, 1997.

Larkin, F. Daniel. *New York State Canals: A Short History*. Fleischmanns, NY: Purple Mountain Press, 1998.

Larrabee, Edward M. *Report of Archeological Excavations Conducted at Saratoga National Historical Park, Schuylerville, New York, from June 8 through June 29, 1959*, 1960. Report on file, Saratoga National Historical Park, Stillwater, New York.

Lee, Ronald F. *The Origin and Evolution of the National Military Park Idea*, 1973. National Park Service Online Book. Retrieved January 19, 2010, from http://www.nps.gov/history/history/online_books/history_military/ nmpidea1.htm.

———. *The Story of the Antiquities Act*, 2001 electronic version of 1970 print edition. National Park Service Archaeology Program. Retrieved January 22, 2011, from http://www.nps.gov/archeology/PUBS/LEE/Index.htm.

Lehnert, Julia. "History of Baltimore's Washington Monument and Surrounding Park," 1998. Retrieved March 23, 2010, from http://terpconnect.umd.edu/~jlehnert/history.htm.

Lentz, Robert A., and Winston C. Williams. *Centennial History of the National Society of the Sons of the American Revolution, 1889–1989*. Paducah, KY: Turner Publishing Company, 1991.

Linenthal, Edward Tabor. *Sacred Ground: Americans and Their Battlefields*. Chicago: University of Illinois Press, 1993.

Lossing, Benson. *The American Historical Record, and Repertory of Notes and Queries, Concerning the History and Antiquities of America and Biography of Americans*. Vol. 3. Philadelphia, PA: John E. Potter and Company, 1874.

———. *The Pictorial Field Book of the Revolution*. New York: Harper, 1851.

Lowenthal, Larry. "The Champlain Canal in Saratoga National Historical Park." Typed manuscript, 2000. Saratoga National Historical Park, Stillwater, New York.

Luzader, John. *Decision on the Hudson: The Battles of Saratoga.* Saratoga, NY: Eastern National, 2002. www.eParks.com.

Mackintosh, Barry. *The National Parks: Shaping the System.* Washington, D.C.: National Park Service, 1991.

Mahlstedt, Thomas F. *Archeological Impact Assessment, Saratoga Monument, Schuylerville, New York, Saratoga National Historical Park,* 1980. Report on file, Saratoga National Historical Park, Stillwater, New York.

Manley, Doris Vanderlipp. *National Register of Historic Places Registration Form: Old Champlain Canal,* 1973. Report on file, New York State Office of Parks, Recreation and Historic Preservation, Cohoes, New York.

McClelland, Linda Flint. *Presenting Nature: The Historic Landscape Design of the National Park Service, 1916–1942,* 1993. National Park Service Online Book. Retrieved November 18, 2009, from http://www.cr.nps.gov/history/online_books/mcclelland/mcclelland.htm.

Mecklenburg Monument Association. *Unveiling of the Monument to the Signers of the Mecklenburg Declaration of Independence at Charlotte, N.C., May 20, 1898.* Charlotte, NC: Observer Printing and Publishing House, 1898.

Moore, Jackson W. *Archeological Exploration of the Neilson Barn Site, Saratoga National Historical Park, New York.* Report on file, Saratoga National Historical Park, Stillwater, New York.

National Park Service. "Bunker Hill Monument." Boston National Historical Park, 2010. Retrieved February 19, 2010, from http://www.nps.gov/bost/historyculture/bhm.htm.

———. *Cultural Landscapes Inventory: Schuyler Estate, Saratoga National Historical Park.* Boston: National Park Service, 2002.

———. "Lexington Green, Massachusetts." Colonials and Patriots: Survey of Historic Sites and Buildings, 2005. Retrieved March 23,

2010, from http://www.nps.gov/history/history/online_books/ colonials-patriots/sitec14.htm.

———. "Prospectus for the Visitor Center and Museum, Saratoga National Historical Park." Typescript manuscript, n.d. Saratoga National Historical Park, Stillwater, New York.

———. "Yorktown Victory Monument." Yorktown Battlefield, 2005. Retrieved February 19, 2010, from http://www.nps.gov/york/ historyculture/vicmon.htm.

New York State Historical Association. *Proceedings of the New York State Historical Association, Seventeenth Annual Meeting.* Vol. 15. New York: self-published, 1916.

———. *Proceedings of the New York State Historical Association, Sixteenth Annual Meeting.* Vol. 14. New York: self-published, 1915.

New York Times. "Acts for Saratoga Park." May 20, 1939.

———. "Army Seeks Views on Saratoga Plan." 1932.

———. "Asks Federal Park at Saratoga Field." February 18, 1937.

———. "Battlefield Work Begun." July 14, 1926.

———. "The Battle Monument Damaged." June 7, 1888.

———. "The Battle of Saratoga. Memorial to Congress for $200,000 to Build a Rival of the Bunker Hill Monument." December 6, 1873.

———. "Dedicate Battle Monument." October 19, 1912.

———. "Delaying the Purchase of Saratoga Battlefield." August 16, 1928.

———. "Drift of Congressional Work." May 3, 1880.

———. "George E. Bissell, Sculptor, Dies at 81." August 31, 1920.

———. "The Monmouth Monument." November 14, 1894.

———. "Move to Restore Field at Saratoga." September 20, 1925.

———. "Mr. Donaldson Wants His Pay." August 15, 1888.

———. "New-London in Early Days, Scene of Many Stirring Events During the Revolution." September 30, 1896.

———. "Noted Sculptor Dead. Jonathan Scott Hartley Succumbs After Long Illness—His Works." December 7, 1912.

———. "Plans to Enlarge Saratoga Park." March 5, 1940.

———. "Proposes Saratoga as a National Shrine." October 18, 1929.

———. "The Saratoga Battlefields Saved." April 16, 1926.

———. "The Saratoga Battlefield." March 19, 1930.

———. "Saratoga Bill Signed, President Approves Survey of the Battlefield by the Government." June 4, 1930.

———. "The Saratoga Monument. Laying of the Cornerstone with Masonic Ceremonies—Speeches by the Hon. Horatio Seymour and George William Curtis—Other Exercises." October 18, 1877.

———. "The Saratoga Monument, Meeting of the Association and Election of Officers." August 12, 1891.

———. "The Saratoga Monument. Plans of the Completed Structure and the Need of Funds." May 19, 1883.

———. "Saratoga Park Bill Approved." April 21, 1938.

————. "Shrine at Saratoga." May 15, 1938.

————. "To Make Last Fight for Saratoga Fund." February 19, 1928.

————. "Urges Saratoga as a Shrine." January 9, 1930.

————. "W.R. O'Donovan Dies." April 21, 1920.

Okey, Paul. "The Champlain Canal in Saratoga NHP, Historic Resources Study." Typescript manuscript, 1995. Saratoga National Historical Park, Stillwater, New York.

Online Encyclopedia. "Ellen Hardin Walworth (1832–1915)–Historic Preservation," 2010. Retrieved April 20, 2010, from http://encyclopedia.jrank.org/articles/pages/4799/Walworth-Ellen-Hardin-1832-1915.html#ixzz0rhmu6ySl.

Oudemool, Lisa, Chistopher Stevens, H. Eliot Foulds, Eric Schnitzer, Linda White and Chris Martin. *Cultural Landscape Report: Saratoga Battlefield, Saratoga National Historical Park*. Vol. 1, *Site History, Existing Conditions, and Analysis*. Boston: Olmsted Center for Landscape Preservation, National Park Service, 2002.

Phillips, Maureen K. *Historic Structure Report: General Philip Schuyler House*. Historic Architecture Program, Northeast Region, National Park Service, 2003.

Phillips, Michael M. "Documented Legislative History of Saratoga National Historical Park." Typescript manuscript. Saratoga, NY: Saratoga National Historical Park, 1973, edited and updated, 1997.

Public Archaeology Laboratory (PAL). *National Register Nomination Form, Minute Man National Historical Park*. PAL Report No. 1010, 2001.

Purcell, Sarah J. *Sealed with Blood: War, Sacrifice, and Memory in Revolutionary America*. Philadelphia, PA: University of Pennsylvania Press, 2002.

Quinn, Judith A., and David Bittermann. *Saratoga Monument Historic Structure Report* (draft), 1992. Report on file, Saratoga National Historical Park, Stillwater, New York.

Radar Solutions International (RSI). *Geophysical Report: Ground Penetrating Radar, Magnetometry, and Electrical Resistivity Investigations at the Victory Woods Sites, Saratoga National Historical Park, Schuylerville, New York.* Prepared for Hartgen Archeological Associates, Inc., the LA Group, and the National Park Service, 2006.

Reeve, Stuart, and Dean R. Snow. *Report on Archeological Investigations and Excavations of Revolutionary Sites, Saratoga National Historical Park, New York, 1974–1975.* Report on file, Saratoga National Historical Park, Stillwater, New York.

Robinson, Christine. "Saratoga Battlefield Monuments." Typescript manuscript, 2005. Prepared by Curator, Saratoga National Historical Park, Stillwater, New York.

Savage, Kirk. "History, Memory, and Monuments: An Overview of the Scholarly Literature on Commemoration." Philadelphia: University of Pennsylvania, n.d. Retrieved January 14, 2010, from http://www.nps.gov/history/history/resedu/savage.htm.

Sawyer, William. "The Battle at Oriska." Fort Stanwix National Monument, National Park Service, 2007. Retrieved June 28, 2009, from http://www.nps.gov/fost/historyculture/the-battle-at-oriska.htm.

———. "The 1777 Siege of Fort Schuyler." Fort Stanwix National Monument, National Park Service, 2007. Retrieved June 28, 2009, from http://www.nps.gov/fost/historyculture/the-1777-siege-of-fort-schuyler.htm.

Sellars, Richard West. *Pilgrim Places: Civil War Battlefields, Historic Preservation, and America's First National Military Parks, 1863–1900,* 2008. Retrieved June 23, 2009, from http://www.nationalparkstraveler.com/2008/08/

pilgram-places-civil-war-battlefields-historic-preservation-and-america-s-first-national-m-0.

Seymour, John F., Ellis H. Roberts, William Dorsheimer and Otto E.C. Guelich. *Dedication of the Oriskany Monument, August 6, 1884*. Utica, NY: Ellis H. Roberts and Company Printers, 1885.

Shimoda, Jerry Y. "The Champlain Canal." Typescript manuscript, 1963. Saratoga National Historical Park, Stillwater, New York.

Snell, Charles. *A Report on the History, Construction, and Social Use of the General Phillip Schuyler Summer House at Schuylerville (Old Saratoga) N.Y.*, 1951. Quoted in NPS 2002b.

Snow, Dean R. *Archeological Atlas of the Saratoga Battlefield*, 1977. State University of New York at Albany. Report on file, Saratoga National Historical Park, Stillwater, New York.

———. *Report on Archeological Identification of the Balcarres and Breymann Redoubts, 1972 Investigations, Saratoga National Historical Park*, 1972. Report on file, Saratoga National Historical Park, Stillwater, New York.

———. *Report on Archeological Investigations of Revolutionary Roads, Saratoga National Historical Park, New York*, 1976. Report on file, Saratoga National Historical Park, Stillwater, New York.

———. *Report on the Archaeological Investigations of the American Line, the Great Redoubt and the Taylor House, Saratoga National Historical Park*, 1974. Report on file, Saratoga National Historical Park, Stillwater, New York.

Sprague, Delos E. *Descriptive Guide of the Battlefield of Saratoga*. Ballston Spa, NY: Battlefield Publishing Company, 1930.

Starbuck, David R. *The American Headquarters for the Battle of Saratoga: 1985–1986 Excavations, Saratoga National Historical Park*, 1987. Report on file, Saratoga National Historical Park, Stillwater, New York.

————. *Saratoga National Historic Park, Archeology Progress Report—1985,* 1986. Report on file, Saratoga National Historical Park, Stillwater, New York.

————. *The Schuyler House. In Saratoga National Historical Park, Archeological Progress Report—1987,* 1989. Report on file, Saratoga National Historical Park, Stillwater, New York.

Stevens, Christopher, Linda White, William Griswold and Margie Coffin Brown. *Cultural Landscape Report and Archeological Assessment for Victory Woods, Saratoga National Historical Park, Village of Victory, Town of Saratoga, New York.* Final draft, April 2007. Boston: Olmsted Center for Landscape Preservation, National Park Service, 2007.

Stevens, Christopher M. *Cultural Landscapes Inventory: Saratoga Monument, Saratoga National Historical Park.* Boston: National Park Service, 2002.

Stone, William Leete. *History of the Saratoga Monument Association.* Albany, NY: Joel Munsell, 1879.

————. *Memoir of the Centennial Celebration of Burgoyne's Surrender, Held at Schuylerville, N.Y., Under the Auspices of the Saratoga Monument Association, on the 17th of October 1877.* Albany, NY: Joel Munsell, 1878.

————. *Visits to the Saratoga Battle-Grounds, 1780–1880.* Albany, NY: John Munsell's Sons Publishers, 1895.

Taft, Lorado. *The History of American Sculpture.* New York: MacMillan Company, 1903.

Taylor, George. *Martyrs to the Revolution in the British Prison Ships in Wallabout Bay.* New York: W.H. Arthur & Company, 1855.

Times magazine. "Names that Make News." July 27, 1931. Retrieved June 21, 2010, from http://www.time.com/time/magazine/article/0,9171,752928-1,00.html.

Todd, Charles Burr. *In Olde New York, Sketches of Old Times and Places in Both the City and the State.* New York: Grafton Press, 1907.

Trenton Battle Monument Association. *Programme: Dedication of the Trenton Battle Monument, October 19th, 1893.* Trenton, NJ: self-published, 1893.

Tuckerman, Bayard. *Life of General Phillip Schuyler, 1733–1804.* New York: Dodd, Mead and Company, 1903.

United States Secretary of State. *United States Statutes at Large.* Vol. 52. Washington, D.C.: Government Printing Office, 1938.

Unrau, Harlan D., and G. Frank Williss. *Administrative History: Expansion of the National Park Service in the 1930s*, 1983. National Park Service Online Books. Retrieved November 18, 2009, from http://www.cr.nps.gov/history/online_books//unrau-williss/adhi.htm.

Walworth, Ellen Hardin. *Battles of Saratoga, 1777; The Saratoga Monument Association, 1856–1891.* Albany, NY: Joel Munsell's Sons, 1891.

———. *Saratoga: The Battle—Battleground—Visitor's Guide.* New York: American News Company, 1877.

Wheildon, William W. *Memoir of Solomon Willard, Architect and Superintendent of the Bunker Hill Monument.* Boston: Bunker Hill Monument Association, 1865.

Whitford, Noble E. *History of the Barge Canal of New York State.* Supplement to the Annual Report of the State Engineer and Surveyor. Transmitted to the legislature on June 30, 1921. Albany, NY: J.B. Lyon Company Printers, 1922.

———. *History of the Canal System of the State of New York together with Brief Histories of the Canals of the United States and Canada.* Supplement to the Annual Report of the State Engineer and Surveyor. Transmitted to the legislature on March 28, 1906. Albany, NY: Brandon Printing Company, 1906.

Wilson, James Grant, and John Fiske. "Jared Clark Markham." *Appleton's Cyclopedia of American Biography*. Vol. 4, *Lodge–Pickens*. New York: Appleton and Company, 1888.

Wood, W.J. *Battles of the Revolutionary War, 1775–1781*. Major Battles and Campaigns Series, John S.D. Eisenhower, General Editor. Cambridge, MA: Da Capo Press, 1990.

Zukowsky, John. "Monumental American Obelisks: Centennial Vistas." *Art Bulletin* 58, no. 4 (December 1976): 574–81. College Art Association.

Themes and currents in American history are always checked with landmark reference, such as the work of Samuel Eliot Morison, and emerging bodies of scholarship, such as that of Dr. Ray Raymond, MBE, DSM and FRSA.

USEFUL MAJOR REFERENCES

Web links and key source points for regional Saratoga history include the following.

Saratoga National Historical Park
648 Route 32
Stillwater, NY 12170
(518) 664-9821, ext. 3.
www.nps.gov/sara

Library of Congress
http://memory.loc.gov

Other rich resources include the following.

The Saratoga Room at the Saratoga Springs Public Library
49 Henry Street
Saratoga Springs, NY 12866
www.sspl.org

The New York State Military Museum and Veterans Research Center
61 Lake Avenue
Saratoga Springs, NY 12866
(518) 581-5100
http://www.dmna.state.ny.us

Saratoga Springs History Museum
Canfield Casino in Congress Park
1 East Congress Street, PO Box 216
Saratoga Springs, NY 12866
saratogahistory.org

Stillwater Historian's office
Box 700
Stillwater, NY 12170
(518) 664-6946
www.stillwaterny.org/town-government/town-historian.asp

Brookside Museum (for related Saratoga County material)
Saratoga County Historical Society
6 Charlton Street, Ballston Spa, NY 12020
www.brooksidemuseum.org

Saratoga County Chamber of Commerce (experiences in the Saratoga
  area)
28 Clinton Street
Saratoga Springs, NY 12866
(518) 584-3255
www.saratoga.org

Results can be readily found on all major search engines such as Google and Yahoo with tags such as "Battles of Saratoga," "Saratoga Battlefield," "Saratoga National Historical Park," "Burgoyne, Gen. Philip Schuyler."

Images can be found on the Internet in instant groupings combining the subject with the term "image" or search option offered on the search engine. There are good collections of images featuring accurate renderings of soldiers and uniforms of the Continental and Revolutionary period, including those offered for purchase, on websites such as historicalimagebank.com.

Important memory keepers include national commemorative societies such as the DAR, SAR and CAR.

Index

Schuyler, General Philip 25, 46, 52,
61, 83, 149
Schuyler House 62, 74, 83, 84, 85,
87, 139, 141
Schuyler, Philip, II 83
Schuylerville (Old Saratoga) 62, 63,
71, 74, 83, 84, 87, 104, 112
Skenesborough 26, 32, 33, 34, 103
Slingerland, George O. 75, 76, 77
Stamp Act 19, 20
Stark, Brigadier General John 35,
52, 53, 111
St. Clair, Major General Arthur 32,
33, 37, 99
Stillwater 36, 37, 63, 74, 79, 95, 97
St. Johns, Quebec 30
St. Leger, Lieutenant Colonel Barry
30, 35, 36
Stone, William L. 62, 63, 64, 92
Strover, George 84
Sutherland, Lieutenant Colonel
104, 105, 107, 108
Sword Surrender Site 135

T

The Battlements (newsletter) 122

U

USS *Saratoga* 131

V

Valcour Island 26, 32
Victory Woods 52, 86, 107
Von Breymann, Henrich 35, 51
Von Rhetz 42
Von Riedesel, Baroness Frederica
100, 103, 105, 112, 113
Von Riedesel, Baron Friedrich
Adolph 31, 32, 33, 34, 40,
42, 45, 47, 48, 49, 50, 52, 53

W

Walworth, Ellen Hardin 66, 68,
149
Washington, George 27, 29, 37, 44,
47, 61, 70, 121, 124
Wilbur's Basin 98, 99, 101, 120
Wilkinson, Lieutenant Colonel
James 49, 57, 99, 105, 108,
109, 117, 120

Y

Yorktown, Virginia 57, 120, 122

About the Authors

Timothy Holmes is a researcher of history who assembled and wrote *Saratoga Springs: A Brief History*, published by The History Press. He writes about locations and themes whose significances have proved enduring over time. His career in philanthropy and forensics continues with humanitarian development projects locally and abroad.

Libby Smith-Holmes assisted in writing and editing *Saratoga Springs: A Brief History* with her husband in 2008. They work together on various local projects, including economic revitalization in Schuylerville, New York, and share an interest in genealogical research that has taken them to England, Ireland, Canada and the eastern United States in pursuit of ancestors. As a writer and editor on environmental topics, she continues to keep an eye on local water quality issues. For one season, she was director of the Youth Conservation Corps at Saratoga National Historical Park. The authors actually met at the Saratoga Battlefield in 1999.

Visit us at
www.historypress.net